Fred
With best wishes
John Manterfield

NEWTON'S GRANTHAM

The Hall Book and life in a Puritan town

Written and edited by John B Manterfield

with additional contributions from

Rob Iliffe
John Down
Ruth Crook

as part of Lincolnshire's Age of Scientific Discovery
A heritage project examining the life and times of Sir Isaac Newton and other Lincolnshire philosophers in the 17th century

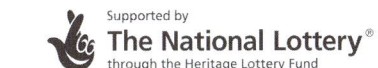

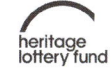

Supported by The National Lottery® through the Heritage Lottery Fund | heritage lottery fund
Supported by the Heritage Lottery Fund

South Kesteven District Council · Grantham Civic Society · U3A The University of the Third Age

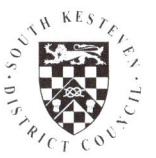

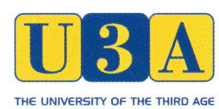

September 2014

Foreword by Professor Rob Iliffe
**Director of the Newton Project,
University of Sussex**

I've been interested for some time in using crowd sourcing to produce material relevant to the life and works of Isaac Newton. Meeting members of the Grantham U3A at the 2012 Gravity Fields festival provided an opportunity to work with U3A members to produce a high quality transcription of the Grantham Hall Book records from the 1650s. This was of particular interest to the Newton Project because the document contains fascinating information about William Clarke, Newton's landlord during the second half of the decade. Publishing this text online will make these records available to a wide audience, and it can serve as an excellent example of what can be achieved by local groups working in the digital medium. The resulting materials can serve as a focus for expanding the already substantial interest in the characters and events that made up the most politically explosive period in Grantham's history.

Contributors

John B Manterfield BA PhD, studied geography and archaeology at Exeter University where, in 1981, he gained a PhD on the topographical development of Grantham. He has written several articles and reviews for Lincolnshire History and Archaeology. With his wife Barbara, he produced the carto-bibliography for volumes 4 and 5 of the Harry Margary facsimile of the Old Series Ordnance Survey Maps of England and Wales. He is currently continuing research on Grantham's early modern and Georgian history.

Ruth Crook is a registered nurse and midwife, who worked as a neonatal ward sister. Her interest in history and genealogy was nurtured by her father, an amateur archaeologist. She has written several local history books and appeared on television and radio, and in Who do you think you are? at The National Archives. She is currently liaising with The National Maritime Museum at Greenwich, which has commissioned a play using her research about an ancestor who fought at Trafalgar.

John Down was a mechanical engineer and managing director of a software house before his retirement. Since then he has been active within U3A at local (Grantham), county and regional level. Of particular interest to him is the life, work and times of Sir Isaac Newton.

Published by the Grantham Civic Society
©Individual Contributors 2014
ISBN 978-0-9929978-2-3

Contents

Introduction John Down 5

Newton's Grantham –
Town Governance and the Hall Book 1649-1662 John B Manterfield

1	The Hall Book	9
2	The Town of Grantham in the Seventeenth Century	9
3	The Corporation	13
4	Civic Culture	18
5	Borough Finances	20
6	Economy and Occupational Structure	23
7	Religion and the Church	25
8	The Grammar School	28
9	Other Corporate Responsibilities	30
10	Conclusion	34
Appendix 1	Courts and Assemblies	37
Appendix 2	List of Aldermen, Comburgesses and Second Twelvemen 1649-62	38

William Clarke – the Man Ruth Crook 41
Grantham Civic Society 44

List of Illustrations

All figures are from the Grantham Hall Book (by kind permission of Lincolnshire Archives and South Kesteven District Council) unless otherwise stated. Other illustrations are copyright of John Manterfield.

Front	Statue of Sir Isaac Newton, St Peter's Hill, Grantham	
Plan of Newton's Grantham		8
Fig. 1	The Grantham Hall Book	9
Fig. 2	Parish, Borough and Lordship Boundaries in Grantham, 1835	11
Fig. 3	Map of Grantham soke from Turnor, 1806	12
Fig. 4	First Court of Thomas Doughty 30 October 1657 folio 310r	15
Fig. 5	Well Lane Mill drawing by Claude Nattes 1796 courtesy of Lincolnshire Library Services	17
Fig. 6	Election of Alderman Robert Trevillian on 22 October 1658 folio 320r	21
Fig. 7	Mill Master's account for 1650-51 7 November 1651 folio 243v	22
Fig. 8	St. Wulfram's Church from the southeast	25
Fig. 9	Agreement for repairs to the steeple 16 July 1652 folio 252v	28
Fig. 10	King Edward VI's Grammar School, Grantham	29
Fig. 11	Appointment of Henry Stokes, Schoolmaster, 11 January 1650 folio 208v	29
Fig. 12	Agreement for lease of Robert Lewin's house in Vine Street, 2 September 1653 folio 264r	31
Fig. 13	The Conduit, Market Place, Grantham	31
Fig. 14	Agreement for maintenance of Conduit by William Palmer, 1 February 1650 folio 209r	32
Fig. 15	Agreement for repairs of streets 4 October 1650 folio 217v	32
Fig. 16	Orders to distrain Richard Branston 8 January 1658 folio 312r	33
Fig. 17	Site of William Clarke's House, High Street, Grantham	42

INTRODUCTION

John Down

This booklet has been produced to coincide with the publication on the Lincs to the Past website at www.lincstothepast.com of a series of transcriptions from the Grantham Hall Book. The Hall Book is the Minute Book of Grantham Corporation, the predecessor of Grantham Borough Council. The earliest volume covers the period from 1633 to 1704 and is kept at the Lincolnshire Archives.

The project to make and publish these transcriptions arose from a series of apparently random coincidences. In 2012 the Gravity Fields Festival took place in Grantham. It was designed to celebrate the town's connection with Newton and the director of the festival invited both local special interest groups and academics from further afield to attend. It was through discussion with the Festival Director that we, a U3A group studying the life, work and times of Isaac Newton, learnt of 'an academic who is looking for someone to do some research locally on a Newton theme'. During the Festival we met the academic: Director of the Newton Project at the University of Sussex, Rob Iliffe, Professor of Intellectual History and History of Science. He explained that, whilst a pupil at the Free Grammar School, now known as The King's School, Grantham, Newton (born at Woolsthorpe by Colsterworth, eight miles south of the town) lodged with William Clarke. Clarke's wife Katherine may have been a friend of Newton's mother. Clarke was a local apothecary who was also a member of Grantham Corporation. Wouldn't it be interesting, Iliffe suggested, to look in the Hall Book to try and gain a measure of this public figure, to find out more about Clarke's character and see if and how he may have influenced the young Newton. Today we know him as an important scientist but Newton was also a theologian, an alchemist, a Member of Parliament and Master of the Mint.

Thus were the seeds sown – but what should be the scope of the project? How and why would it be published? How would it be undertaken, co-ordinated, monitored and funded?

We know that Newton lodged with Clarke from 1655 to 1661 and that Clarke was a member of the Corporation from 1649 to 1662. Bill Couth had already produced an edition of the Grantham Hall Book for Lincoln Record Society (Volume 83, 1995) covering the period 1641 to 1649. Thus it seemed sensible to follow on from Couth and transcribe the period 1649 to 1662 to cover both the whole of the time that Newton lodged with Clarke and Clarke's full period as a member of the Corporation.

Looking at similar transcription projects we noticed that The Newton Project at the University of Sussex aims to publish on-line transcriptions of all Newton's writings, whether published or not, at www.newtonproject.sussex.ac.uk . The University of Cambridge holds a large and valuable collection of Newton's papers, especially scientific ones, and images of these are available at www.cudl.lib.cam.ac.uk/collections/newton. So it was clear that on-line publication should be an aim, and so too should hard print, following in the footsteps of Couth.

A team of people willing to transcribe the Hall Book was recruited from U3As throughout Lincolnshire. The University of the Third Age (U3A) is a self-help educational charity for 'those no longer in full time employment'. At the time of writing there are more than 800 U3As in the UK, 26 in Lincolnshire and one in Grantham. With a scoped project and a team of volunteers it was possible to create a plan and to attract funding as part of South Kesteven District Council's (SKDC) Lincolnshire in the Age of Scientific Discovery programme from their Heritage Lottery Fund grant. This funding has provided training for the transcribers, administration of the project and the production of this booklet.

The relevant pages of the Hall Book were photographed and made available to all the project team members who then completed their transcription independently. Accuracy of transcription has been a key aim of the project and careful checking has been essential. The original document was hand-written in ink more than three hundred years ago. A number of different clerks were involved, even within the same year, and some hands are clearer than others! In places ink blots obscure passages and bleed-through from the other side of the page is a frequent problem, as seen, for example, in Figure 7. Unusual words, forms of English, abbreviations, word endings and superscripts were all additional challenges for the team, as was the problem of inconsistency. In the original document words and names appear with different spellings, often in the same paragraph; the use of upper case letters is haphazard; and so is the use, or lack, of punctuation. The project team has faithfully recorded all these inconsistencies in the so called 'literal' transcriptions.

In an effort to ensure that the difficulties inherent in the original texts did not affect the production of accurate transcriptions, we adopted the following protocol. Each year has been transcribed by one member only – but some members have transcribed more than one year. Each transcription has been checked by another team member, returned to the original transcriber who then decided which suggested changes to make before offering the document for further checking by a second team member. Upon return, the original transcriber had full say again over which changes and corrections to make to his or her work. Some folios have had additional checks where discrepancies could not be resolved within the prescribed protocol.

For the on-line publication the transcriptions have been 'normalised' and edited by one team member, Dr John Manterfield, to produce an edition that is uniform in appearance and consistent in the application of transcription rules with each word written in full. A short note on the editorial method appears below. Each transcript occupies one page as per the original, and is displayed opposite an image of the original. It is therefore possible to compare the two directly.

Whilst transcripts for the years from 1649-50 to 1654-55 have been published initially on-line, it is expected that by the end of 2014 all years up to and including 1661-1662 will be available on the website. At least some years in the literal transcription will also be published on the same website. It is hoped to publish the normalised version in print later.

Following this Introduction are two essays. The first, by Dr John Manterfield, is an exploration of Newton's Grantham using a range of examples illustrative of the discussions and decisions of the Alderman's Court (or Council Meeting). The second, by Ruth Crook, concentrates on William Clarke's life and family. These essays set the scene and the context within which the Minute Book was written. They do not aim to provide a full commentary on the period covered by these transcriptions or an analysis of the texts; neither do they aim to provide a definitive history of Grantham in the period.

Online Editorial Method

The on-line edition appearing on the Lincs to the Past website has the original image of each folio of the Hall Book on the left-hand side and the transcription on the right-hand side in a pdf format. Readers are therefore expected to use their computer zoom facilities to read the texts. Readers may also search for words or names using the Edit Find facility. Font sizes vary according to the number of words on the individual folios of the Hall Book. Dates have been given in Old Style with the year beginning on 25 March. The language of the Hall Book is English with the headings of some Courts given in Latin although dates have been standardised in English. Less well known Latin words have been translated and shown in square brackets. Some continuation folios are headed in Latin, for example 'adhuc sexta Curia A... B..., Aldermani', which has been retained but may be translated as 'Still the sixth Court of A... B..., Alderman' and so forth. A majority of Courts end with 'By the Court' or in Latin 'Per Curiam'.

The transcription reproduces the original spelling except that missing words have been supplied and abbreviations silently expanded where their meaning is certain. The 'thorn' has been replaced by 'th'. The use of the letters 'i', 'j', 'u' and 'v' has been standardised. Punctuation has been modernised but capital letters have been retained as in the original. Personal names and abbreviations for forenames have been transcribed as they appear with exact spellings. Monetary sums have been given in either arabic or roman numerals as in the original and are standardised as 'li s d'. Italics have been used for the marginal notes given in the Hall Book which generally summarise accurately the body of the text which, in the transcription, follows immediately below. The editor has attempted to follow the advice given in R F Hunnisett, *Editing Records for Publication* (British Records Association, 1977).

Acknowledgements

This project has been funded by the Heritage Lottery Fund. The Project Team is grateful to the Grantham Civic Society for agreeing to become the publisher of this booklet. Images of the Hall book and its contents are reproduced by kind permission of Lincolnshire Archives and South Kesteven District Council.

The Project Team wishes to thank the following for their encouragement, help and support:

Rosemary Richards and Ameneh Enayat, Project Directors for Lincolnshire's Age of Scientific Discovery
Debbie Nicholls, collation and Rachel Thirde, design, South Kesteven District Council for assistance in the design and production of this booklet
Professor Rob Iliffe, University of Sussex
Dr Mike Rogers, Collections Access Team Leader, Lincolnshire Archives
Dr John Young, University of Cambridge, for training, checking and advice
Dr David Crook for checking and advice on publication
Mrs Ruth Crook for checking transcripts and contributing an essay to this booklet
Dr John Manterfield for his transcriptions, checking, essay, editing and unfailing enthusiasm
Mrs Barbara Manterfield for the preparation of the on-line published material
Miss Costanza Pearce for checking transcriptions
Mr Trevor Goodale, Grantham U3A, for photographing the Hall Book.

I wish to record my special thanks to the team of transcribers:

Joanne Bramwell, Branston & District U3A
Jan and Nigel Christmas, Louth U3A
Patience Gibb, Wellingore & District U3A
Josephine Hewitt, Grantham U3A
Dr John Manterfield, Grantham U3A
Anna Mauro-Pearce, Grantham
Jackie Searl, Bourne U3A
Elaine Thurgood, Bailgate & Lincoln U3As
Dr Amanda Topp, Sleaford U3A

John Down, Grantham U3A
Project Leader.

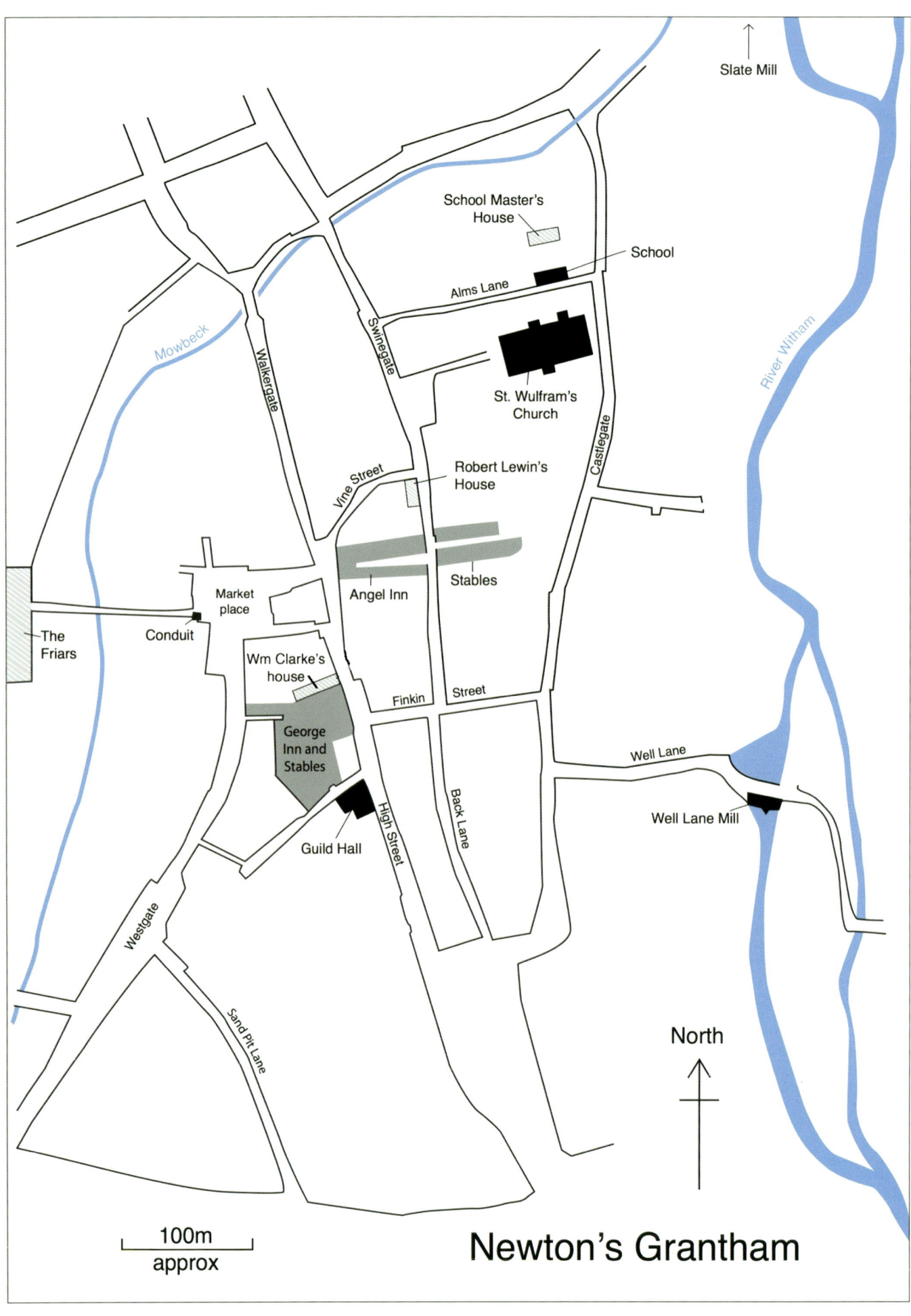

NEWTON'S GRANTHAM - TOWN GOVERNANCE AND THE HALL BOOK 1649-1662

John B Manterfield

1. The Hall Book

The earliest surviving book of minutes recording the discussions and decisions of the Alderman's Court of the Corporation of Grantham covers the period from October 1633 to October 1704 and is known as the Hall Book. The volume, which now belongs to the Corporation's legal successor, South Kesteven District Council, is in the care of Lincolnshire Archives.[1] This work relating to the period 1649-1662, covering broadly the period when Newton was at school in Grantham, spans therefore less than a fifth of the period covered by the Hall Book. Specifically, the section covered in the on-line transcription covers folios 204 to 369 out of a total of 780 that form the volume. The volume is made up of paper sheets, written in English with some headings in Latin, with a leather binding. It measures approximately 43.5 cm by 28.5 cm and is 11.5 cm from cover to cover (Figure 1). Owing to the span of years, the volume reflects the handwriting of at least seven different Clerks. On some sheets, the ink has bled through leaving occasional small portions of the text illegible.

It is clear that during the time when the surviving Hall Book was being used, there existed at least five earlier minute books which are now lost.[2] These may have extended from the time of Grantham's Charter of Incorporation in 1463.

2. The Town of Grantham in the Seventeenth Century

What, then, would the young Isaac Newton have seen in Grantham whilst lodging in the High Street with William Clarke? What do we know of the town's layout, its streets and buildings and how big was the town both in terms of population and its physical extent?

The borough of Grantham itself covered an area of less than two-thirds of a square mile lying in the centre of the larger ecclesiastical parish of Grantham centred on the church of St Wulfram. The borough was bounded on its eastern side by the River Witham which flows north towards Lincoln before turning south-eastwards towards Boston and the Wash. The western and northern boundary of the borough was the stream known as the Mowbeck which rises to the southwest of Grantham in Harlaxton. The borough's southern

Fig.1 The Grantham Hall Book (Lincolnshire Archives – Grantham Borough 5/1)

boundary was the line of what is now known as Wharf Road and St. Catherine's Road. To the southwest lay Earlsfield which by the seventeenth century had become a separate liberty or manor but was perhaps originally part of the medieval manor of Grantham. To the south was the manor of Spittlegate, Houghton and Walton and to the east extending between the River Witham and the line of the Roman Ermine Street or High Dyke was the manor of Harrowby. To the north and northwest of the borough was the manor of Little Gonerby cum Manthorpe. These contiguous manors and liberties that surrounded the old borough at its core all formed part of the parish of Grantham. One small and extra-parochial area immediately on the west side of the borough was known as the Grange and comprised the former site of the Franciscan house known as the Friars or Greyfriars. The complexity of local boundaries is evident from the map drawn up in the 1830s as part of the evidence for the reform of municipal corporations (Figure 2).

In Newton's time, the Earlsfield area had largely been enclosed into a number of arable and pasture closes whereas most of the land in Little Gonerby and Manthorpe to the north of the town and in Spittlegate, Houghton and Walton to the south of Grantham comprised unenclosed open fields with open heath land used for grazing in the higher areas. Parts of Harrowby were unenclosed but it is possible that some enclosure had already taken place by the 1650s.

The Corporation of Grantham had jurisdiction not only over the area of the old borough but also over the soke of Grantham, which included the villages of Barkston, Belton, Londonthorpe, Manthorpe, Great Gonerby, Denton, Harlaxton, Great Ponton, Braceby, Sapperton, Stoke Rochford, Easton and Colsterworth (figure 3).[3] With the soke's origins dating back to the late Saxon period and recorded in Domesday Book, Grantham's charter of Incorporation of 1463 confirmed that the town's Alderman and Comburgesses were to be the "Justices to preserve and enforce the peace within the said town or borough, the soke, boundaries and liberties of the same". This particular privilege was amongst several that were jealously guarded by the Corporation which resisted any attempts to infringe any of its liberties and responsibilities. In October 1654, eight men were alleged to have violated the town's privileges and the Alderman's Court agreed that legal action be commenced against them.[4]

The street pattern in 1650 was broadly that which has survived today and reflects a pattern that had become well established by the late fourteenth century. Surviving medieval documents and property deeds confirm the names of the principal streets. Walkergate (now Watergate) continued into High Street as the main north-south axis that formed the Great North Road from London to York. Along this axis were the Angel and George inns and other taverns serving the needs of travellers.

Running roughly parallel and to the east was Elmer Street (then also known as Elmer Lane or the Back Lane) and Swinegate and further to the east lay the line of Castlegate which in turn was broadly parallel to the River Witham. These three axes converged at the south end of the borough on what is now St. Peter's Hill and where, until less than a decade before, had stood the Eleanor Cross. To the west of the junction of High Street and Walkergate, and opposite the Angel Inn, lay the Market Place with its market cross and water fountain known as the Conduit which had supplied the town with water through lead pipes from Barrowby fields for over 300 years. Adjacent to the Angel Inn, at the opening for Vine Street, was Coal Hill where the town's coal market was based.

Running southwest from the Market Place was Westgate, initially a narrow street with its burgage plots running off at the rear towards the Mowbeck stream. The street then opens out into wide Westgate which was used for fairs and an overflow for the market. Connecting these north-south axes were Finkin or Finkle Street running from opposite the George across to Castlegate and also Vine Street which ran north-eastwards from near the Angel into Swinegate, Alms Lane ran from Swinegate and crossed on the north side of the church into Castlegate. Here stood, and survives today, the Grammar School attended by Newton.

Before the churchyard was extended in c1838 a number of cottages stood in Church Pavement up to within 10 metres of the west door of the church.[5]

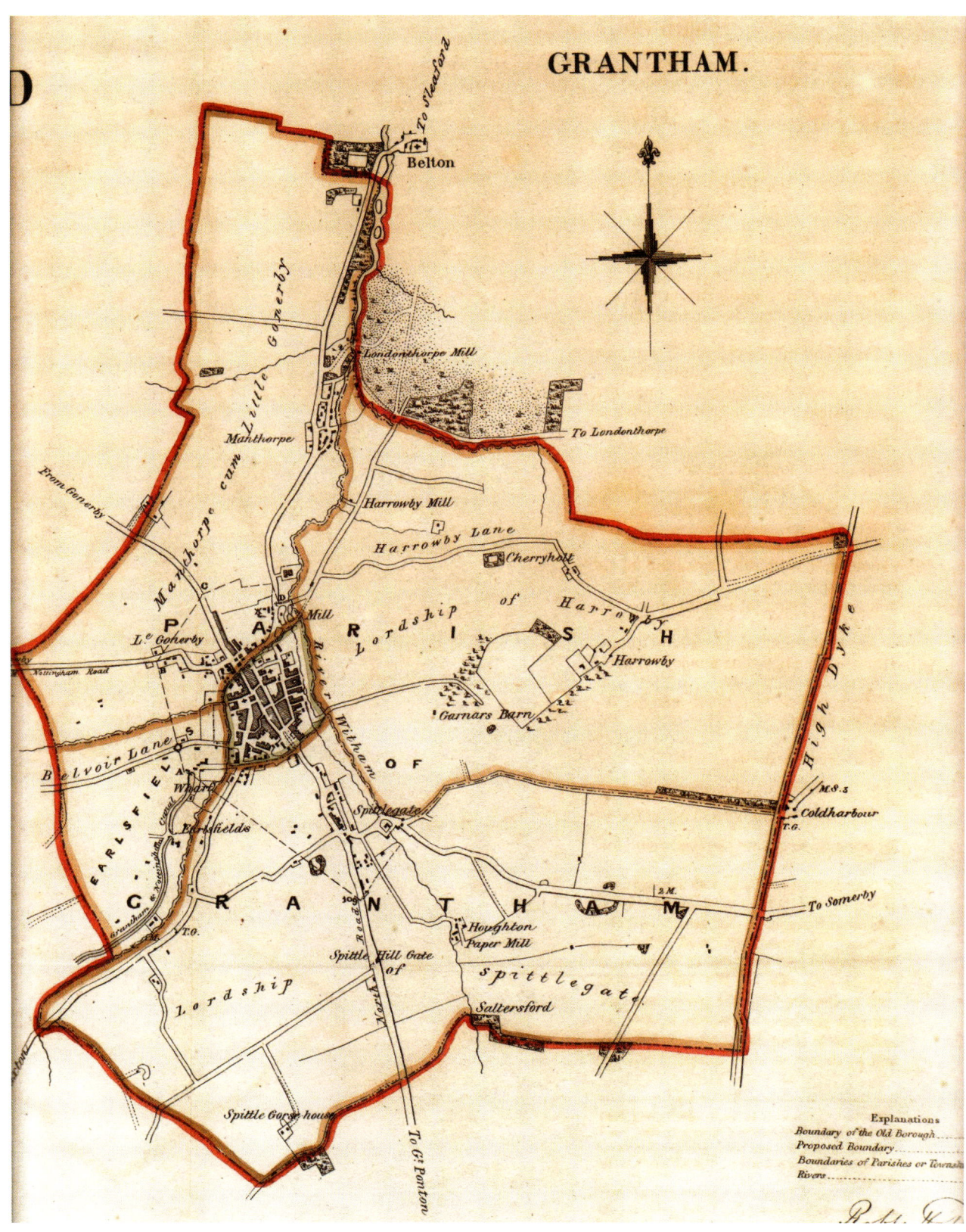

Fig.2 Parish, Borough and Lordship boundaries in Grantham, 1835

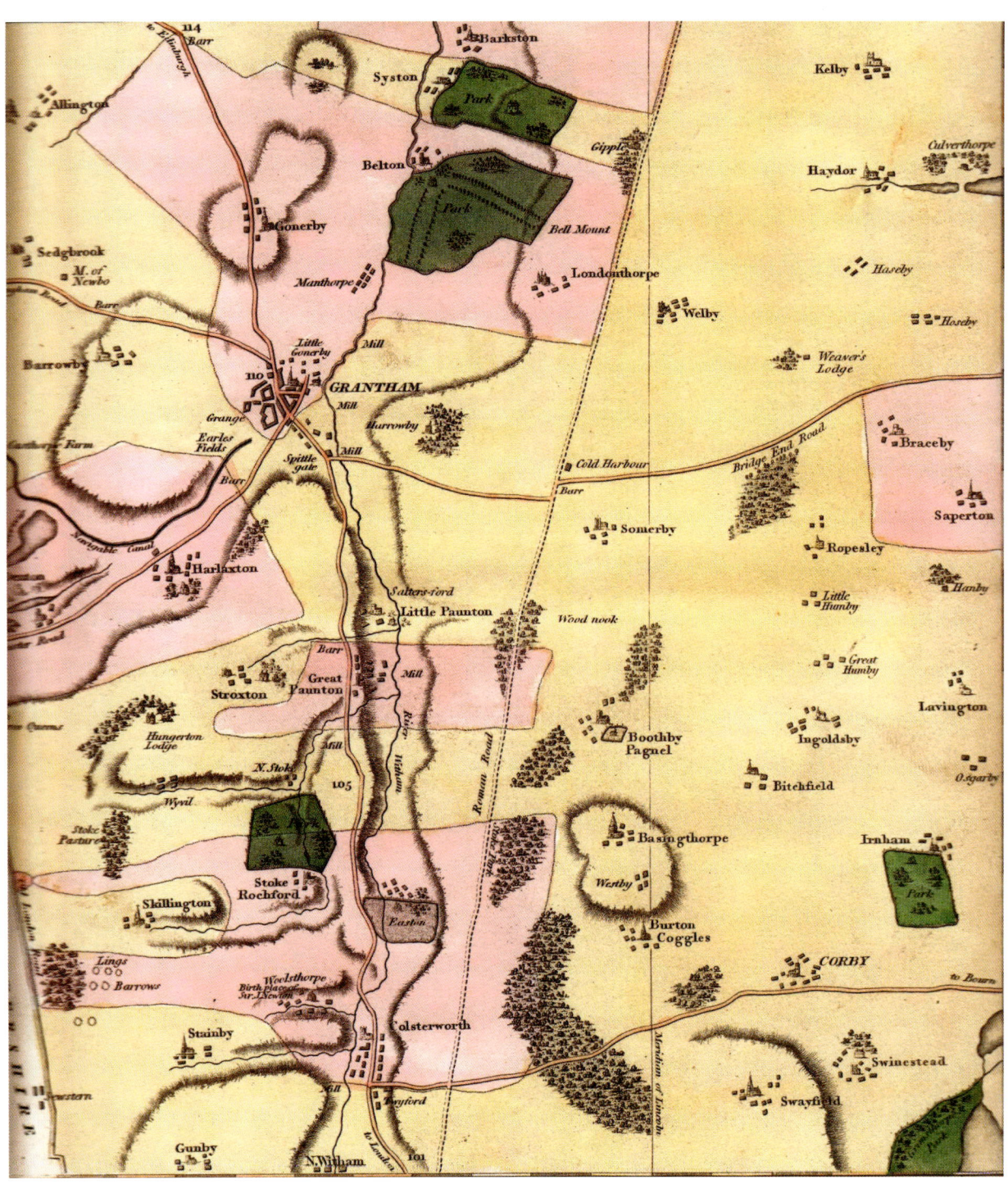

Fig.3 Map of Grantham soke from Turnor, 1806
The parishes that formed the soke are shown in pink.

The town in the 1640s had a population of some 1800-2100 people housed mostly within the old borough. This population estimate is inferred from the Liber Cleri return of 1603 which reported 1008 communicants. Allowing one third of the town's population to be children, then this would indicate a total of over 1500 persons and if the proportion of children was 40% then the total would be nearly 1700 persons. The Compton Census of 1676 records a total of 1460 persons over the age of 16, indicating a total of 2190 people assuming one third were children or 2430 if that proportion was 40%. The best estimate for the 1650s is therefore between 1800 and 2000 people.[6] Owing to the interruption of Grantham Parish registers between October 1643 and December 1658, it is not possible to be more accurate and the presence at various times of troops may have temporarily swelled the population. Evidence from the Hall Book shows that civic leaders were concerned about the harbouring of strangers or inmates within the town. Such concerns were in part grounded by issues of overcrowding and fear of disease. Early seventeenth-century Grantham had witnessed severe epidemics of plague in 1604, 1617, 1625 and 1637. The worst outbreak between June 1604 and March 1605 resulted in over 320 burials, that is, about one fifth of the town's population. The Corporation's pest house in Manthorpe fields, established in 1584, could not prevent epidemics neither could the repeated orders, recorded in the Hall Book, for householders to cleanse the streets and remove rubbish.[7]

The short-term effects of the plague were dramatic; trade was disrupted, markets and fairs and the Alderman's Courts were suspended. On 5 July 1637 the Corporation petitioned the Privy Council "shewing the greate distresse and miserie into which the said Borough is lately fallen, by reason of the Infection of the Plague amongst them, and complayneing in particular that diverse of the better sorte of freemen and Members of that Towne have thereupon left theire habitacions there; whereby the Government and Well ordering of those remayneing especially of those that are visited becomes a greater burthen than otherwise it would be".[8] The Privy Council ordered that the justices for the county raise an assessment for relief with any inhabitants who had fled being charged at twice the rate. The Corporation was also empowered to order any of its officers back if this was thought necessary.

3. The Corporation-Historical background

Corporate boroughs, such as Grantham, owed their status to their royal Charters of Incorporation and to subsequent confirmations and additions of privileges in letters patent issued by successive monarchs. In the case of Grantham, Edward IV's charter of 8 March 1463 gave the town corporate status and established its Alderman (thereafter elected annually) and twelve Comburgesses. The term Alderman is one that was used in a number of boroughs, including Stamford, and was the equivalent to mayor as the town's leading citizen. Less commonly used amongst corporate boroughs is the term Comburgesses, meaning fellow burgesses, which in Grantham was given to the First Twelve members who, together with the Alderman, formed the magistracy or Justices of the Peace. As a corporate borough, the town had powers to sue and be sued, to acquire and dispose of land, to renew its membership, make by-laws and use a common seal. Not only were the Alderman and Comburgesses invested with the Commission of the Peace for the town and soke, the Charter also excluded various royal officials such as the purveyors of the King's Household from acting within the town. Richard III's charter of 3 March 1484 granted the town the rights to a Wednesday market and two annual fairs, although it is possible that the grant may have merely confirmed existing arrangements.[9]

Tudor monarchs successively confirmed these earlier grants and Queen Elizabeth's surviving charter of 1559 preserves the texts of the six lost originals. Two other royal grants deserve mention. In 1553, Edward VI refounded the grammar school and endowed it with lands from the former chantries of the Holy Trinity and the Blessed Mary and other rent charges. The ongoing management of the school estate is reflected in the discussions of the Corporation in the mid-seventeenth century. In 1597, Elizabeth granted the borough the right to appoint its own Escheator and specifically confirmed the town's immunity from the county Escheator. The wording of the grant, however, indicates that, in practice, the Alderman and Burgesses had already been accustomed to appointing an Escheator "to do and perform all that pertains to be done to the office of escheator".[10] During the 1650s, the Escheator's duties appear mostly to have related to defective weights and measures rather than holding inquisitions post mortem and certifying to the Exchequer details of those estates where landholders and tenants of crown estates had died without heirs. James I, by his charter of June 1604, authorised a wool market to provide funds for the relief of the poor and to provide stocks of wool for weaving. James's charter also extended the Corporation's jurisdiction by allowing a weekly civil Court of Record for the recovery of debts up to the value of £40. Although the Charter granted this power, it appears that the Court of Record or Pleas was not established at this time as the Corporation returned to discussion of implementing this power in October 1650.[11] The legal framework and structure of the town's Corporation was further clarified and confirmed through the charter of Charles I dated 30 November 1631. For the first time in a Charter text, the Alderman's Court was specifically referred to and the Alderman and 12 fellow Comburgesses, that formed the First Twelve, were seen to act with a Second Twelve and the other Burgesses in the choosing or removing of any Comburgess (for any notable cause) and in the making of laws, statutes, ordinances and constitutions for the 'general good and utility' of the town. Provision was also made for a Deputy Alderman to act if the Alderman was sick, incapacitated or absent from the town and the grant of 1631 also refers to the Council's Common Clerk. It is therefore this Charter that has shaped the structure of the Corporation that operated within Newton's Grantham and that has given the framework for the earliest surviving minute book, known as the Hall Book, for the period 1633 -1704.[12]

Structure and Officials

Each year on the Friday next after St Luke's Day (18 October), an Assembly was held in the Corpus Christi Choir of St Wulfram's Church at which the Alderman for the coming year was elected and took his oath of office. The choice of this location for the Alderman's election ceremony was a tradition that almost certainly dated back to the medieval Corpus Christi guild which was in existence by 1339.[13] On the Friday following the election of the Alderman, the first Court of the year was held at which the First and Second Twelves and Commoners were sworn in. The Commoners of the Court were listed according to the wards in which they dwelt or held property. During the period from 1649 to 1661 the number of commoners listed in the Alderman's inaugural Courts ranged from 27 for Thomas Doughty in 1657 to 42 for Gilbert Chantler in 1661 and the average was just over 31. The names of all Aldermen, Comburgesses and Second Twelvemen who served in the period 1649-1662 are given in Appendix 2. At these inaugural Courts the various officers and officials were also appointed and sworn accordingly (Figure 4). The Courts were held in the Guild Hall (usually referred to as the Common Hall) which stood in the High Street at the southern corner with modern-day Guildhall Street - the present Guildhall on St. Peter's Hill was not built until 1869-70.

The roles of the named officials of the Court deserve some explanation. The Coroner was always a Comburgess and traditionally the most recent Alderman. His duties were broadly similar to those of a modern Coroner in carrying out inquests into unexplained or sudden deaths and also whether by virtue of that death anything accrued to the town.

The Escheator was also a Comburgess, often recently appointed to the First Twelve. His duties as noted above included holding inquisitions post mortem to ascertain whether any lands should escheat or revert to the crown if the tenant or landowner had died without heirs or heirs who had reached their majority. In Grantham, he also accounted for receipts in respect of fines for defective weights and measures.

The Hall Book also names the two Churchwardens who normally served for overlapping periods of two years. It is unclear whether the naming of the Churchwardens, one of whom was usually a Second Twelveman, implies that their actual appointment took place by and in the Alderman's Court or whether they had been chosen previously at a meeting of parishioners or Vestry and were endorsed as a matter of record in the Corporation meeting.

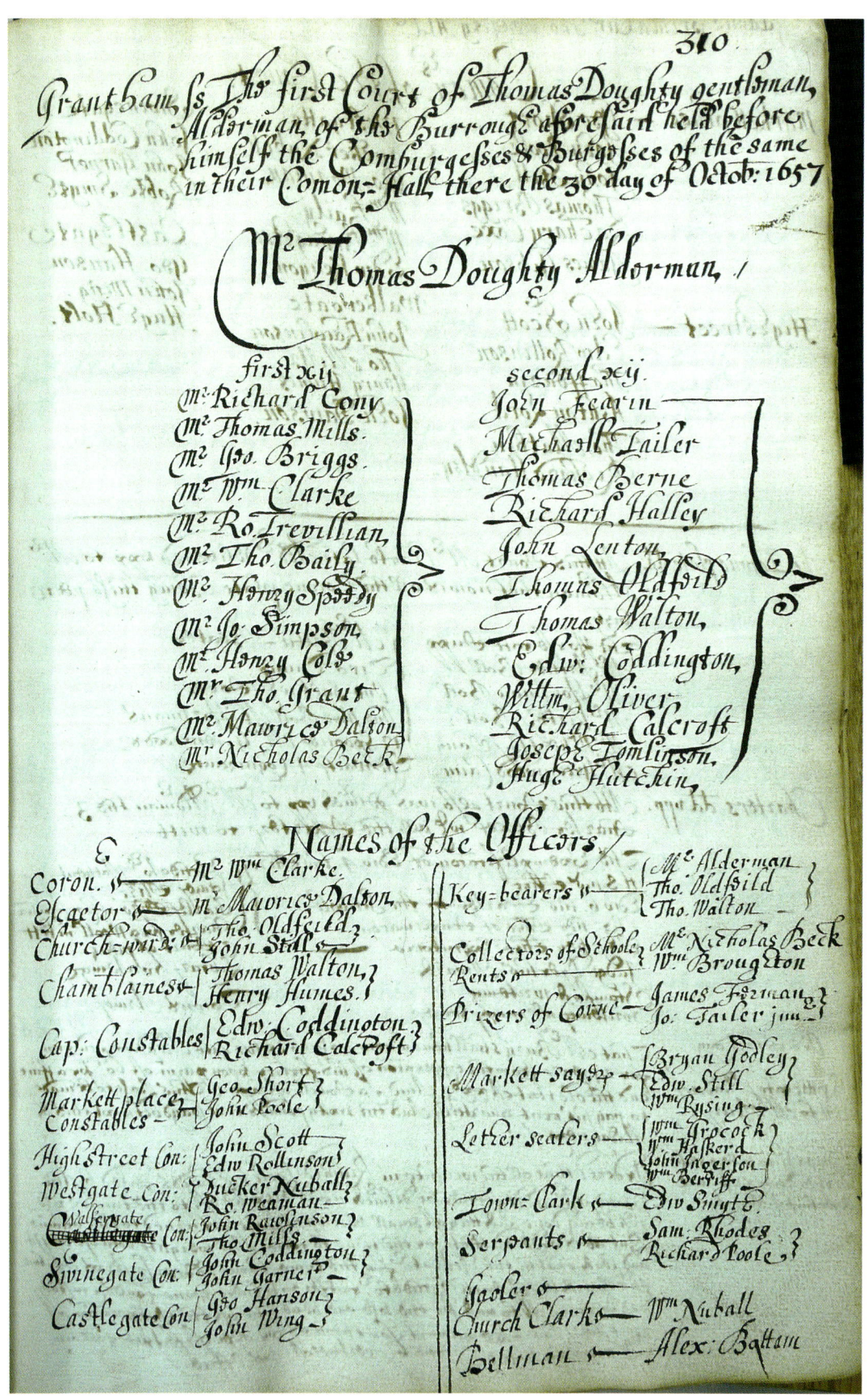

Fig.4 First Court of Thomas Doughty, Alderman 30 October 1657 – Folio 310r

The two Chamberlains were effectively the borough's Treasurers. They had an onerous workload receiving in monies from other officials and assessors appointed to raise monies for specific purposes and making disbursements as directed by the Court. The absence of a formalised banking system, a chronic indebtedness on the part of the borough and a shortage of small change did not make their jobs any easier as cash received for particular purposes was often applied to meet pressing payments. One Chamberlain was normally a member of the Second Twelve, the other a Commoner and it was usual for this office to be held only for one year at a time.

The Alderman's Clerk or Town Clerk was not a member of the Corporation but an appointee who had probably had formal legal training and business experience. Eleven clerks served the town between 1633 and 1693 including the appropriately named Robert Clarke appointed in 1639 but dismissed in 1649 due to age and disability of body. He was succeeded by Edward Smyth who held office from November 1649 to 1658. Smyth's successor was Henry Hall, admitted Town Clerk in December 1658, but within 18 months he had died and was succeeded by William Hodgkinson in May 1660.[14]

The two Chief or Capital Constables were usually relatively experienced members of the Second Twelve and they appear to have held a supervisory role over the twelve Petty Constables, two for each of the borough's six wards. The Petty Constables were Commoners who had the unenviable tasks of collecting in assessments such as for the repair of wells or pumps in their own wards or as part of borough-wide collections for repair of roads, repairs to the church and steeple or raising monies to repay the town's debts. Another duty was the collection of goods where inhabitants had been distrained for breaching the borough's regulations or ordinances. Tickets were issued by the Court to the Constables, for example, if a Commoner was absent from Court or a person was reported for trading whilst not being a Freeman. The Constables were also asked, for example, to go out and check who was setting work for tailors who were unfree and foreign, that is, not free-born or from Grantham. From time to time, Constables were threatened with legal action for executing their duties and the Court agreed to hold them harmless and indemnify them.[15] To contemporary eyes therefore, the Constables may be viewed as the enforcers of the Corporation's policies and by-laws. Each Constable was equipped with a halbert, presented by William Welby in 1651. Constables were also expected to oversee the stock of hooks, ladders and buckets which formed the town's rudimentary fire-fighting equipment.[16]

The two Serjeants-at-Mace, referred to in the earliest charter of 1463, attended the Alderman in Court and were the Mace bearers in civic processions. During the seventeenth century, one of the Serjeants was frequently the town's gaoler and probably resided adjacent to the gaol cell at the rear of the Guildhall. The role was also combined with that of Bailiff of the Liberties; Richard Poole, for example, had the three roles between 1642 and 1653.

Each year, three persons were appointed as Key Keepers to the Common Hutch. The Hutch, a wooden chest with three iron locks with separate keys, was kept in the Church. One key holder was the Alderman, another was one of the Church wardens and the third was one of the two Chamberlains. The Hutch contained documents (although the royal Charters themselves were kept in a green desk) and ready money, although this appears to have been in short supply. The town's plate may have been kept in the hutch too when not required for use by the Alderman.

Three other groups of named officials, appointed annually, deserve mention. The two Collectors of School House Rents comprised one Comburgess and one Commoner. Their role was to collect in the rents from over thirty properties with which the Grammar School was endowed and to pay the salaries of the Schoolmaster and the Usher and any other disbursements related to the management of the school estate (see below). As with other officials, their accounts were presented annually at the close of the Aldermanic year. The Corporation also appointed four Mill Masters, two for each of the town's water mills, namely Slate Mill and Well Lane Mill (Figure 5). Again a Commoner was usually paired up with a Member of the First Twelve and together they gathered in the income from grinding corn and met the disbursements in respect of the upkeep of the fabric of the Mills and Mill banks. A further role was probably to ensure that flour was not adulterated and sacks were accurately weighed.

Fig.5 Well Lane Mill (drawing by Claude Nattes c1796) (courtesy of Lincolnshire Library Service)

A third group of officials were appointed annually with roles akin to present-day consumer protection. Four leather sealers ensured the quality and grading of leather at various stages of production. Two Prizers or Pricers of Corn set the price of wheat, barley, oats and rye at the times when harvests could be variable. Prices could also be affected by variations in water supply to the mills. The Corporation appointed up to three Market Sayers who enforced market regulations and may have collected market tolls and determined the positioning of market stalls. One person who also held office but was not annually appointed was the town's Recorder, "a discreet man learned in the laws of England" as expressed in the 1631 Charter.[17] The Charter recognised that there could also be "some sufficient deputy". In the 1630s, the recorder was George, seventh Earl of Rutland, but he died in 1641. His heir, the eighth Earl, was a distant cousin who spent more time at Haddon Hall than at Belvoir Castle.[18] The Corporation chose Mr William Ellis, a lawyer, born in Grantham to be its Recorder following the death of the seventh Earl. Ellis became an MP for Boston in 1640 and his re-appointment as Recorder was confirmed on 8 October 1647. The Corporation noted he had been Recorder for five years past and "of whose faithfullness and abilities wee have had sufficyente testimonies". Ellis became Solicitor-General for Cromwell from 1654, a post he held until 1660 and was one of the MPs for Grantham in 1656 and 1659. Ellis' advice was sought by William Clarke over the re-establishment of the Court of Pleas in 1650. Ellis resigned his office of Recorder in January 1662.[19]

The Composition of the Corporation 1649-1662

The membership of Grantham's Corporation in the period 1633 to 1649 has been described in detail by Bill Couth who also edited the Hall Book for the years 1641 to 1649 for publication by the Lincoln Record Society.[20] Following ordinances of Parliament dated 9 September and 4 October 1647, the Alderman's Court expelled all those who had been in arms against Parliament or aided or assisted them. Royalist Comburgesses Edward Rawlinson, Edward Christian, George Lloyd and Robert Calcroft were dismissed together with Thomas Short and William Cole of the Second Twelve and three Commoners also stood down on 17 September 1647. Comburgess Alexander More was dismissed on 28 September and Comburgess Gilbert Chantler and Second Twelveman Thomas Secker were dismissed on 8 October 1647. Four more Commoners were dismissed for aiding the enemy on 21 October. Other burgesses, who had not been members of the First and Second Twelves and were listed in the Hall Book as Commoners, may have also quietly absented themselves when the Corporation was purged of royalists. Comburgess Arthur Rhodes resigned through age on 21 October. The changes, however, opened up opportunities for a number of others to have a relatively rapid rise to holding office as Comburgesses or as members of the Second Twelve. William Clarke was promoted to the First Twelve on 24 September 1647, Thomas Doughty was also promoted to the First Twelve on 1 October 1647 and Robert Trevillian was likewise promoted on 20 August 1648, all three having only moved from being Commoners to the Second Twelve on 16 October 1646. Their rapid advancement continued as Clarke served as Alderman for the year from 1 November 1650, Doughty succeeded him on 31 October 1651 and Robert Trevillian in turn succeeded Doughty on 29 October 1652.[21] The borough's governing body in the 1650s was clearly younger and less experienced than that of a decade earlier. It is more difficult to judge whether it was more radical in its outlook and actions or whether it was more inclined towards Puritanism.

Clearly changes in membership continued during the 1650s as some of the First Twelve died, moved away or were dismissed. Clarke, Doughty and Trevillian each served second terms as Aldermen from October 1656, 1657 and 1658 respectively.[22] Whereas in Grantham, town governance may have appeared settled during the later 1650s, major changes were afoot nationally. In September 1658 Lord Protector Oliver Cromwell died and was succeeded by his son Richard. The Protectorate was at an end and Charles II was proclaimed King on 8 May 1660. The Alderman, Comburgesses, Second Twelve and Commoners were required to sign the oath of Supremacy and Allegiance which the majority did on 8 June 1660 with a handful not doing this until January 1661. In March 1661, the Corporation received a writ of Mandamus requiring them to inquire into the membership and restore those who had been removed in the time of the late troubles. Five men, Richard Pearson, Robert Calcroft, Edward Christian, Gilbert Chantler and Christopher Hanson were re-admitted through the voluntary resignation of others including Robert Trevillian who stood down in favour of Richard Pearson. Thomas Doughty had died before March 1661 and his vacant place was taken by Gilbert Chantler on 22 March. In June, four others, Mr Thomas Short, John Watson, Thomas Hanson and Edward Watson desired to be readmitted. Two men were asked to leave in accordance with a royal commission headed by Sir William Thorold and both resigned on 3 October 1661. These were William Clarke whose place was taken by Richard Calcroft and Maurice Dalton whose place was taken by Thomas Short. Thus, by the first Court of Alderman Gilbert Chantler on 1 November 1661, the restoration of nine men had been completed. However, under the Act for Well Governing and Regulating of Corporations 1662, a Commission of six local gentry required Corporation members to take an oath and to subscribe their names in accordance with the legislation. Two Comburgesses (George Briggs and John Simpson) and one Second Twelveman (Mathew Wythey) declined to subscribe. Four Commoners also did not respond to the summons and all seven men were dismissed on the orders of the Commission held on 27 August 1662. This process brought to an end the reform of the Corporation following the restoration of Charles II.[23] In this, of course, Grantham was typical of borough corporations as well as other public institutions across the country where supporters of the Parliament were purged just as royalists had been purged 15 years previously.

Analysis of the membership of the First and Second Twelves and Commoners from the 1650's (Appendix 2) shows that the town's governing body (totalling 55-60 men) formed a small proportion of the town's population, perhaps ten percent of the town's adult male population (see section 2 above). Labourers, apprentices, servants and paupers had no franchise and the exclusion of Royalists and anyone who had supported forces opposed to Parliament reduced further the pool of members that formed the ruling elite. In this, again, Grantham typified corporate towns and cities across the country.[24]

4. Civic Culture

The Hall Book from 1633 consistently demonstrates the status given to the Alderman and Comburgesses that formed the First Twelve. The headings for each Court describe the Alderman as gentleman and he is referred to as Mr Alderman with other Comburgesses referred to by their names as 'Mr'. In contrast, members of the Second Twelve and Commoners are mentioned by their Christian and family names. A similar treatment is found in the parish registers from the late sixteenth century, where the description Comburgess is occasionally added.[25] In this regard, therefore, the town's ruling elite were given the status of gentry even though many had achieved membership of the First Twelve having risen through promotion from the ranks of Commoners and through the Second Twelve of the Court. On Court days, usually

Fridays, and also when attending Church, First Twelve members wore their cloaks and may have carried staffs. The Bell Man acted as Town Crier summoning members to meetings in the Common or Guild Hall and, when requested, walked the town to warn townspeople that unclaimed goods taken as distresses would be sold.[26]

Despite the upheavals in membership in 1647 and again in 1661, the Court's decisions as reflected in the Hall Book present, more often than not, a model of unanimity and consensus. The phrases "by an unanimous consent" or "by a general consent" are repeated frequently even when one might have expected this not to be the case. There are few recorded examples of votes having been taken. At one level, this unanimity may be seen as the borough reflecting the good instrument of the state, preserving order and modelling good governance. Civic leaders were well aware of their roles in taking decisions for the common wealth and public good so as to preserve the peace and prevent disorder. In so doing, they avoided potential scrutiny and intervention from the Privy Council or from county officials and they preserved the independence of the borough. By the same token, what was done, in terms for example of the Alderman, the First and Second Twelve and Commoners swearing their oaths of office at the start of each Aldermanic year, reinforced corporate loyalty to serve the Alderman. Oath-taking represented an important rite of passage in civic culture in early modern England as individuals progressed up the civic hierarchy. Although the exact wording of the oaths taken by newly-admitted Freemen in Grantham does not survive, the form of words used in Stamford is indicative of what would have been expected in Grantham.

"You shall swear, that you shall be true, and true Faith bear to our Sovereign Lord the King that now is, his Heirs and Lawfull Successors; and to your Power you shall aid and assist the Mayor of this Borough of Stamford, and his Successors, Mayors of the same for the time being; and to them and every of them you shall be obedient and attendant, concerning all Things as they or any of them shall reasonably and lawfully will and command you to do. You shall also well and truly observe, perform, fulfil and keep all such Orders, Rules and Cositutions <sic> as are or shall be made and establish'd by the Mayor, Aldermen and Capital Burgesses of this Town and Borough, for the good Government thereof, in all Things to you appertaining. You shall also give, yield and become Contributary of this Town, so far forth as you ought or shall be chargeable to do. And you shall not, by colour of your Freedom, bear or cover under you, any Foreign Person or Stranger; nor shall you complain for any Remedy to any Person or Persons, without the Knowledge and License of the Mayor of the Town and his Successors, Mayors of the same, and their Brethren: But according to the best of your Wit, Power, and Skill, you shall uphold and maintain all the Liberties, Franchises, good Customs, Orders, and Usages of this Corporation; and the Counsel of this Town shall well and truly keep. So help you God."

Newly-admitted Grantham Freemen paid their fees and "took their oaths according to auncyent and lawdable custome". This phrase is used to describe the oath taken by the Alderman following his election in the Corpus Christi Choir of St Wulfram's Church (Figure 6).[27] The fees paid 'into the box' were 2s 6d for free-born freemen and 5s for foreigners who had completed their apprenticeships. The officials, the Clerk and two Serjeants, received 6d each from free-born freemen and double that from those not born in the borough.

The Corporation was empowered to appoint its Comburgesses who held office for life although Charles I's charter of 1631 envisaged that they, at their own special request to the Alderman or for any notable cause, could be removed by the Court. During William Clarke's aldermanship, Richard Elston was dismissed from the Second Twelve on 17 October 1651 after having been indicted for fornication with Ann Lord, his servant. In the 1650s, Comburgesses Richard Sheppardson, James Gibson, Edward Bristow, John Wythey, John Rawlinson and Edward Towne all died in office. Thomas Matkine resigned "on account of his age and want of sight" and John Hanson was dismissed "at his earnest desire" on the same day, 7 June 1650.[28] When the Court sought to appoint John Wythey as next in line of the Second Twelve to Hanson's vacancy, he was granted time to consider but was sworn in on 20 September. Prolonged absence from the Court or a move out of town also led to Comburgesses being removed from their office. John Bee, who had been a Comburgess since 1647 and served as Alderman for the year 1648-49, was notably not sworn at the first Courts held in October 1651 and subsequently. On 21 September 1655, it was recorded that "Mr John Bee is knocked of from being of the first Company for that he hath long discontinued and foure yeares out of the Towne att Folkingham".[29] It is unclear what were the precise reasons for Bee's absence but is it mere coincidence that the absence spans the years when William Clarke, Thomas Doughty and Robert Trevillian were Aldermen? Was their agenda too radical? Had there been differences of opinion? Occasionally the Hall Book hints at disagreement and discord. On Christmas Eve 1649 under James Gibson's Aldermanship, the Clerk recorded that "Divers proposicions were made for the proceeding in & settleing of severall Businesses then in Agitacion & of publique concernment but noe business being fully Concluded upon the Court adjourned". In May 1657, whilst William Clarke was Alderman, the Hall Book records that at his ninth Court "The Court being sumoned assembled & called and on Entry upon some particuler businesse being made, certaine differences ariseing by reason that Mr Alderman tooke into his hands and keeping the paper of the last Courtes proceedinges and Orders and refused to deliver them back to the Clarke of the Court to be read confirmed and entered, the Court hereupon dissolved".[30]

5. Borough Finances

One constant theme demonstrated in the Hall Book between 1649 and 1662 is that of corporate debt. On 10 October 1649 'the townes debts were read & openly made knowne amounting to the summe of two thousand pound & upwards' and it was agreed that £2000 would be borrowed from four men, Dr Hurst, Mr William Welby of Denton, Mr William Clarke and Mr Robert Trevillian. In return, it was initially proposed that the town would repay £200 per year for 21 years which Dr Hurst suggested could be reduced to £190 if the men could be freed from all local taxes and assessments.[31] This was not acceptable to Clarke and Trevillian. The men were to be given the profits of the Town's Mills as security. Other debts still required repayment and the Hall Book reveals further monies being borrowed to meet payments and debt charges as they fell due. Such borrowings were done either on bond or on the firm promise of the Court.

The Court's officials were expected to account for their income at the end of each Aldermanic Year. The last Court of the Aldermanic year is sometimes referred to as the Count Day. Officials presented written statements for the year on a 'charge and discharge' system stating what they were charged with in terms of their expected and actual income. The statements then show what they had disbursed less any arrears or other debts and then what was paid into the Chamberlains hands in the case of any surplus income. Conversely, the accounts show the agreed amount that they would be repaid by the Chamberlains. At times, the Court determined to make payments by raising monies from those present with the clear expectation that members of the First Twelve would (in general) contribute more than members of the Second Twelve who in turn would contribute more than Commoners. In some cases, the accounts are recorded in tabular form in the Hall Book in some detail, in others they are summarised by reference to Bills of Particulars which had been presented to the meetings. Once the accounts were read and monies paid in to the Chamberlains, or repaid to the officeholders, then the latter were discharged by the Court (Figure 7).

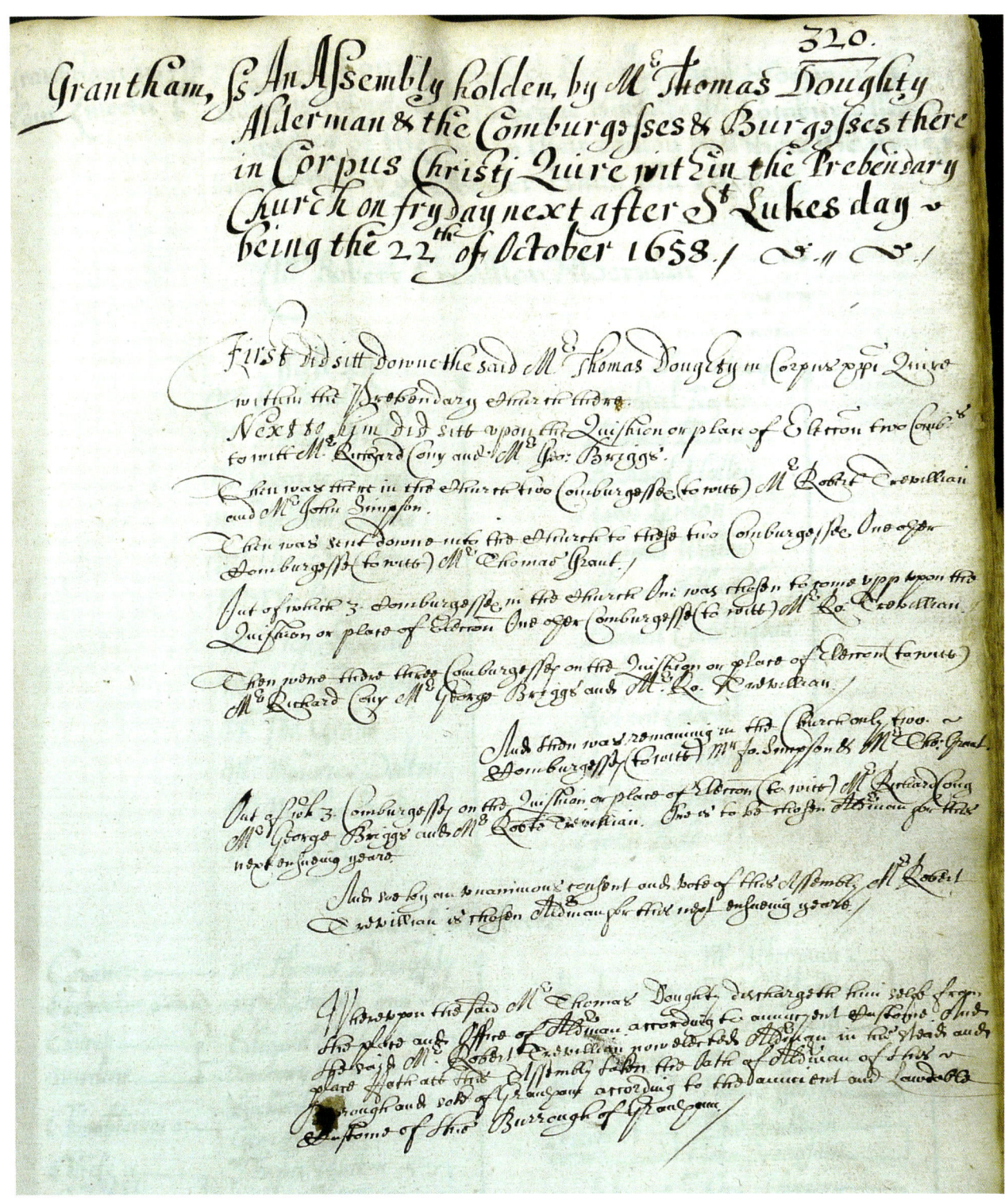

Fig.6 Election of Alderman Robert Trevillian in Corpus Christi Choir 22 October 1658 – Folio 320r

First did sitt downe the said Mr Thomas Doughty in Corpus Christi Quire within the Prebendary Church there. Next to him did sitt upon the Quishion or place of Eleccion two Comburgesses to witt Mr Richard Cony and Mr Geo. Briggs. Then was there in the Church two Comburgesses (to witt) Mr Robert Trevillian and Mr John Simpson. Then was sent downe into the Church to these two Comburgesses One other Comburgesse (to witt) Mr Thomas Grant. Out of which 3. Comburgesses in the Church One was chosen to come upp upon the Quishion or place of Eleccion One other Comburgesse (to witt) Mr Ro. Trevillian. Then were there three Comburgesses on the Quishion or place of Eleccion (to witt) Mr Richard Cony, Mr George Briggs and Mr Ro. Trevillian. And then was remaining in the Church only two. Comburgesses (to witt) Mr Jo. Simpson and Mr Tho. Grant. Out of which 3. Comburgesses on the Quishion or place of Eleccion (to witt) Mr Richard Cony Mr George Briggs and Mr Roberte Trevillian. One is to be chosen Alderman for this next ensueing yeare. And soe by an unanimous consent and vote of this Assembly Mr Robert Trevillian is chosen Alderman for this next ensueing yeare.
Whereupon the said Mr Thomas Doughty dischargeth him selfe from the place and Office of Alderman according to auncyent Custome. And the said Mr Robert Trevillian now elected Alderman in his stead and place Hath att this Assembly taken the Oath of Alderman of this Burrough and soke of Grantham according to the auncient and Lawdable Custome of this Burrough of Grantham.

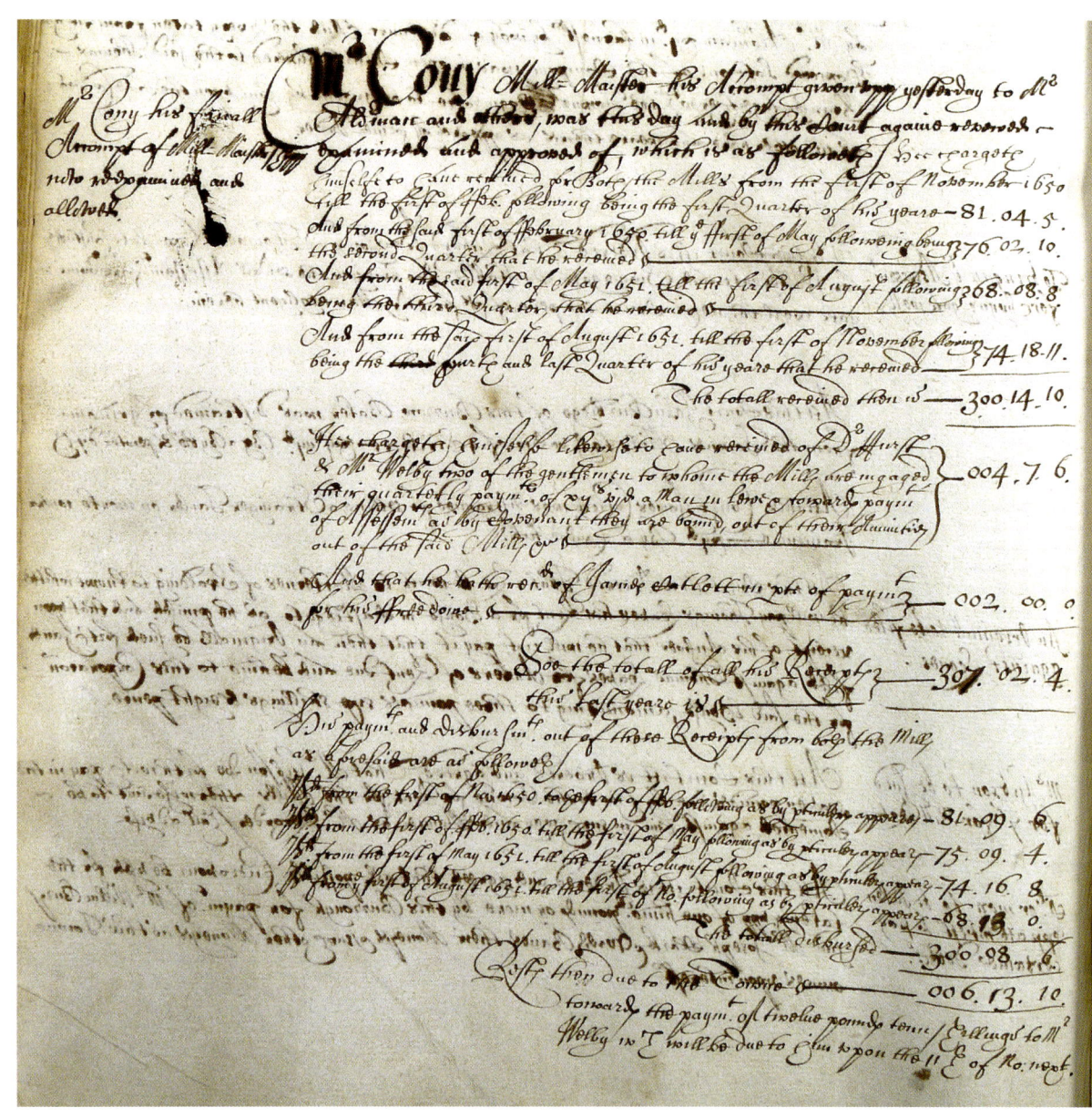

Fig.7 Mill Master's Account for 1650-51 Folio 243v

Needless to say, disputes arose periodically between officeholders and the town and in many cases were referred to a smaller group comprising say two Comburgesses, two Second Twelvemen and three Commoners to resolve. In some cases, a resolution was reported back to the Court; in others, legal action was threatened. When assessments had been agreed to cover particular expenditure such as the repair of a well, it was customary that they would be delegated to a Second Twelveman and a Commoner to collect. When householders did not pay up, then the Court issued tickets to the Petty Constables to distrain goods to the value of the sum due to the town. Goods could be redeemed on payment of the sums due or were sold off after due notice had been given. Petty Constables were clearly caught in the middle with neighbours either unable or unwilling to pay and the Court threatened to fine Constables ten shillings or distrain them for their negligence in not collecting what was due. In November 1654 Constables were being asked to distrain the previous year's Constables. In December, the Constables claimed they were unable to find goods to distrain or that doors were locked against them. They were given further time but the process of gathering in arrears seems to have dragged on for months, although by November 1655 most of the outstanding accounts had been cleared.[32]

One characteristic of the 1650s and 1660s was the chronic shortage of small change. Tokens to the value of a farthing or a halfpenny were issued by a range of shopkeepers bearing their names and frequently the dates of issue. During Newton's time at school in Grantham, tokens were issued by William Clarke, Gilbert Chantler, Henry Cole, Thomas Doughty, Henry Humes, Andrew Poole, Robert Trevillian and Thomas Walton. Other shopkeepers as well as the Overseers of the Poor also issued tokens dating from the 1660s. Compared with other Lincolnshire towns, the proportion of tokens issued in the 1650s was much higher in Grantham. Newton would, inevitably, have been familiar at first hand with the tokens circulating in the town and particularly in Clarke's shop.[33]

6. Economy and Occupational Structure

The Hall Book gives evidence of the occupations of those admitted as freemen. All were men aged 21 years or more who gained their freedom by right of patrimony (their fathers being free born), by apprenticeship (they had served 7 years as an apprentice to a Freeman Master in Grantham) or by purchase. The latter was rarely exercised in the 1650's. In all cases fees were payable to the Common Box and to the Clerk and Serjeants. The fee for foreigners who had not served an apprenticeship was £10, but this was sometimes remitted in part or in whole. The Alderman's Court was therefore able to control who traded in the town. In September 1655, for example, William Oliver of the city of Lincoln, a woollen draper, came to the court and desired his freedom. This was, unusually, put to the vote and 'thought in the negative'. At the next court of 5 October he returned and it was 'taken into consideracion though he be a meere strainger yet in that there are but two woollen drapers in this Borough where there may well be three without prejudice to their trade'. Oliver then paid his £10 and was made free.[34]

When freeman tailors petitioned the Alderman's Court in April 1650, tickets were issued to distrain five foreign tailors as well as those who had set them work. One of these foreign tailors, Jeffrey Hyde or Hynde, was warned again in September 1651 and a third time in January 1657 when he was to be 'discharged'. Although he appears to have eluded the Corporation's control, other tailors and weavers who were warned in September 1651 chose to comply as five were made free in October, together with a shoe maker, a saddler, a butcher, a cooper and an apothecary. Analysis of the admissions to freedom, together with evidence of occupations[35] shown in inventories taken after the deaths of Grantham's inhabitants, gives a good picture of the occupational structure of the town in the first half of the seventeenth century (Table 1).

The town was dominated by the leather trade which included skinners, fellmongers, tanners, curriers, glovers, saddlers, bridle makers, cordwainers, shoemakers and translators. These trades accounted for a quarter of the admissions of freeman and one in five probate inventories. Both the Tanners and the Shoemakers had their own social fraternities. The Tanners met in the Guild Hall and were periodically chased by the chamberlains for rent owed and the Company of Shoemakers had a constitution reputedly granted by Henry VIII.[36] The leather trade not only reflected the importance of cattle-rearing in the local agricultural economy but also the provision of saddles and bridles for travellers and their horses. The four leather sealers appointed annually ensured the grading and quality of the leather produced in the borough.

The second largest occupational group was that related to food and drink, including inn holders, tapsters, bakers and butchers and this in part reflected Grantham's position on the Great North Road. The distributive trades, including mercers, drapers, ironmongers, apothecaries, chandlers and haberdashers, were almost as numerous as the food and drink sector, closely followed by the number of gentry. Gentry of course were not obliged to become Freemen of the Corporation as they were not following a trade. Those gentlemen who were granted freedom in 1660-61 included several whom the Corporation wished to reward or recognise for their loyalty or indeed their potential benefit to the Corporation, for example, William Welby of Denton, John Newton of Heydour and Erasmus Deligne of Harlaxton granted freedom in April 1660. Richard Brownlow, Esquire, was freed in January 1661 and, two months later, William Mountagne, Esquire, was made free 'upon the recommendation of the Earl of Rutland'.[38]

The Corporation's attempts to control who practised their trades within the borough represent a further strand in its attempts to control who settled within the town. The taking in of 'inmates' and harbouring of strangers prompted concern about the growing number of poor people. This led to the Borough issuing ordinances in 1635 based on a copy of orders they had received from Nottingham. The Alderman's Court noted.

"Forasmuch, as it is found by daylie experience, that by the continuall building and erecteing of new Cottages, small Tenements & pore habitations, and by the Convertinge of Barnes, Stables Killnhouses, out-houses, and such like building to habitations & dwelling, And the frequent takeinge in Inmates into the houses of th'inhabitants within this Towne that a great Confluence and resort of poore people from foraigne partes is and have beene occaisioned, and the number of them much increased to the great sur-charge and over-burthening of th'inhabitants of the better sorte within the said Towne, By meanes whereof sundry inconvenyences and greviances have risen within the said Towne not only in regard of the insupportable burthen of the daily Charge and mayntenance of soe great of poor and indigent

Table 1 The Occupational Structure of Grantham[37]

	Admissions to freedom 1644-63		Probate Inventories 1650-99	
	Number	%	Number	%
Gentry	13	6.4	16	16.2
Professional	8	3.9	6	6.1
Distributive	18	8.8	16	16.2
Agriculture	0	0.0	8	8.1
Textiles/clothing	19	9.3	5	5.0
Leather	50	24.6	20	20.2
Food and drink	24	11.8	17	17.2
Building	7	3.4	5	5.0
Metal	7	3.4	2	2.0
Miscellaneous	0	0.0	4	4.0
Sub-total	146	71.9	99	100.0
None recorded	57	28.1	0	0.0
Total	203	100.0	99	100.0

persons, but the said towne hath beene thereby also exposed to great daunger in time of visitation by pestilence or other infecious diseases, which have bene founde to have much dispersed & increased through the disorderly and unruly demeanours of such necessitous and needy people, whoe are hardly restrayned from wandering abroad in such dangerous times of infection, and alsoe much Idleness hath bene thereby increased in the said Towne but alsoe the neighbouring townes about it."[39]

These concerns in relation to inmates continued into the 1640s and 1650s and constables were asked to ascertain the names of strangers and inmates living in their wards.[40]

The control exercised by the Corporation over who traded or lived within the town was also matched by its attempts to protect its corporate privileges from outside interference. This was demonstrated in March 1655 when it was agreed to provide money for a case at Lincoln Assizes against one Barraclough, 'a Forraine baly' for acting within the soke without authority. In February 1657, one Jeremiah Oliver Richard Barroclough (most likely the same man) and Robert Kellam were to be sued for infringing the liberties of the borough by serving of writs and arresting men and either Mr Thornton or Mr William Harvey of Lincoln was to be employed as solicitor for the town.[41]

7. Religion and the Church

On Sundays, attendance at worship in the parish church of St Wulfram (Figure 8) was a legal requirement in mid-seventeenth-century Grantham. Although all the congregation were members of the Church of England as the established church, some were adherents of Archbishop Laud and of Arminianism with its emphasis on sacramental ritual and liturgy, ceremony and music. Others felt there should be much more emphasis on preaching and the study of scripture and striving for personal salvation. The latter group, termed Puritans by their opponents, saw themselves as Godly, with a focus on high personal standards working towards an ideal of protestant perfection. Their beliefs were marked by an intensity of conviction, by self-examination and a refusal to compromise with sin. This was the group that dominated the composition of the Corporation in the period during which Isaac Newton was at school in Grantham. The purging of the Alderman's Court as a result of Parliamentary Ordinances resulted by October 1647 in the loss of sixteen royalists, whom we would reasonably expect to have held religious convictions that were more in support of Laud and Arminianism. This group of royalists comprised several who had been brought before the Committee for Compounding and had been fined for their delinquency. Accordingly, the town's government was thenceforward in the hands of a largely Puritan oligarchy for whom the way was open to help build a new Jerusalem, answerable to both Parliament and to God. From the time of Richard Cony's appointment as Alderman for his second term, a range of actions can be seen to have taken place in line with Puritan beliefs and values which promoted the 'Common wealth' and 'Publique good'. These actions included the appointment of, and ongoing support for, a Godly minister for the town; the re-introduction of weekly lectures, the appointment of a new schoolmaster to promote the Free Grammar School, attempts to set the poor at work through a Manufactory and the more effective regulation of tradesmen and a drive against idleness and support for the deserving poor. These individual actions formed part of a process that was supported by the majority of Corporation members.

Fig.8 St. Wulfram's Church, Grantham from the southeast.

For many Corporation members in Grantham, a defining moment had been in 1627 when an unseemly scuffle took place in the Church between members of the Corporation, led by Alderman Thomas Wicliffe, and the vicar Peter Titley, who, without consultation, had repositioned the altar table from the nave, where it had stood on an east-west axis, to against the east wall of the chancel on a north-south axis. Titley was an adherent of Arminianism and wanted the altar in the chancel to be railed around and accessible to the officiating clergy. The Alderman wanted the table closer to the nave. Following the scuffle, both parties headed off, fifty miles south along the Great North Road, to seek a ruling from the bishop of Lincoln at his palace at Buckden. Bishop Williams, having deliberated carefully, gave a diplomatic response in writing to the Alderman stating that the standing of the Communion Table was 'unto him a thing so indifferent, that unless offence was taken by the town against it, I should never move it or remove it.' He concluded 'Which side soever, you or your parish, shall yield to the other in this needless controversy, shall remain, in my poor judgment, the most discreet, grave, and learned of the two.' It appears that the altar table remained in the chancel even after Titley's death in 1633.[42] The positioning of the altar table, however, reared its head again in 1640 in the context of another matter – the installation of a new organ to which the Puritans objected. A group of Puritans petitioned Parliament on both issues in April 1640 and this was passed to Archbishop Laud. The Alderman's Court, then under royalist influence, submitted a certificate to Archbishop Laud supporting the new organ and the positioning of the altar table. Needless to say, Parliament and the Archbishop had bigger issues to consider and the organ appears to have been used for firewood when the town was occupied by soldiers.[43]

For centuries, the parish church of St Wulfram had been served by the two vicars of North and South Grantham, called in Latin, Grantham Borealis and Grantham Australis. These vicars were instituted as deputies of the prebendal canons of Grantham Borealis and Grantham Australis of Salisbury Cathedral which had been granted lands by Bishop Osmond in 1091. These prebendal holdings in and around Grantham were significant in terms of the tithes due to them, but were relatively small in terms of the physical extent of their lands. A terrier of the South prebendal estate in 1635, let for £30 per year, describes a close of two acres, a barn of six bays and an adjoining piece of ground near the church, with three acres of land in Houghton Field. This prebendal tithe barn was presumably the one built by Richard Aleyne under the terms of his lease of 1545. The North prebendal estate had a two acre close and a barn north of the church with lands in the fields of Gonerby and Manthorpe as described in the terrier of 1638 with the rent then being £33 per year. Both estates had been leased, thereby assuring a steady income for the prebendal canons without the need to collect tithes locally or farm the lands directly. The leases were for the terms of three lives so that by 1650 when the lands were subject to parliamentary survey, there was only one life remaining on both leases. John Still was the prebendal canon of Grantham Borealis from July 1613-May 1662 and Humphry Henchman had been the canon for Grantham Australis from 1623. He later became Bishop of Salisbury from 1660 to 1663 and then Bishop of London until his death in 1675. During the English Civil War, both prebendaries however were deprived of their livings and, in 1649, Parliament passed the Act for the sale of the lands of Deans and Chapters. Serving as the deputies of the prebendary canons in Grantham were their two vicars. Edward Dix had become vicar of South Grantham in 1639 and was almost immediately censured by the then Alderman's Court for not wearing a hood whilst going about his duties. He appears to have been moderate in doctrine and remained in his living up to his death in 1669. The vicar of North Grantham, Thomas Dilworth, had been appointed in 1608 at the approximate age of 28. Despite pawning his books in 1634 and being presented in 1638 at the ecclesiastical court for fornication with Mary Mills, he retained his post until his death in 1646.[44]

In addition to the ministry of the vicars, the town's population had been treated to weekly lectures by "divers worthie & revered divines wherby there hath bine much comfort receaved by their ministrye". These had been interrupted by "these troublesome tymes of warres" and in December 1646 Alderman Richard Cony proposed that letters be written to nine local ministers to reinstate the lectures.[45] Street notes that these lectures were held in the parish church on a Tuesday and that the Alderman and his brethren proceeded to them in state and that a dinner was held with a 'pint of sack' provided for the Lecturer. In 1649 the dinners were to be held at the George but after the inn holder complained that there was insufficient profit for him, it was agreed that the Alderman should entertain the lecturer at his own house.[46]

When vicar Thomas Dilworth died in 1646, it was agreed by the corporation that Mr Thomas Redman, a well-known Lincolnshire lecturer, should be vicar of the town and a petition made to Parliament to establish him in the vicarage. His appointment had been secured through Alderman Richard Cony's contact with Mr William Bury, leader of the Parliamentary Committee in the County, who lived at the Friars in Grantham but also practised at Gray's Inn. Cony also advised Grantham's two MPs of the proposed appointment. In January 1649 it was further agreed that Redman should receive the tithes and annuities lately belonging to Mr Dilworth's vicarage. In July 1650 29 members of the court, eleven of the First Twelve, seven of the Second Twelve and 11 Commoners, individually pledged various sums totalling £10 18 s 8d in lieu of tithes to be paid towards Mr Redman's salary. Nearly half of this total came from six individuals – Comburgesses William Clarke, Thomas Doughty and Robert Trevillian each paid £1 and Alderman James Gibson and Comburgesses Richard Cony, Henry Ferman and Richard Sheppardson paid 10s each. Those that God had blessed were expected to provide for the common good of the parish and provide for their minister.[47]

In January 1650, the Corporation agreed to petition the London Mercers' Company to try to secure a share in the bequest made under the will of Viscountess Campden to provide for the maintenance of two ministers in the counties of Lincolnshire, Yorkshire or Durham. It was agreed that William Clarke take this petition up to London. In March, the Corporation agreed to ask Mr William Bury to go to London to pursue this petition and also to ensure that the £63 combined rent of the seized prebendal estates was directed towards the town's Minister. He was thirdly asked to move the Committee for Plundered Ministers to allow the Corporation to have the nomination for gathering up the tithes at Grantham, Londonthorpe, Spittlegate, Houghton and Harrowby for the benefit of the town's minister. In July, the Alderman's court ordered that Mr Bury be solicited to perfect the petition to the Mercers' Company for the yearly maintenance of a 'painefull Minister for this Towne of Grantham'. In February 1651, William Clarke, then Alderman, went to London with William Bury and they were indeed successful in persuading the Mercers' Company to use one half of the endowment for the benefit of Grantham. Reporting this back to the Alderman's Court on 7 March 1651, the clerk recorded 'All which extraordinary Love care & paines of Mr Alderman & Mr Bury this Court doth well approve of and with an unanimous & thankfull expression accept'.[48] Street states that Rev John Angel was the first Minister appointed by the Mercers' Company to Grantham in 1651. Initially, a contribution was made by the Corporation towards Mr Angel's house rent. When he died in 1656, they appointed Mr Dix, one of the vicars. In September 1662, the Court petitioned the Mercers' Company for the continuance of endowment and agreed to send Comburgess Andrew Broom to London with horse and manservant at all convenient speed.[49]

In addition to trying to ensure that Grantham's parishioners were well cared for spiritually, the Corporation took responsibility for the physical fabric of St Wulfram's church. During the early period of the Civil War when Grantham changed hands and was garrisoned by soldiers, some of whom used the prebendal tithe barn, the church suffered. Allegedly pews and wainscoating were used for fuel and windows were broken. In September 1645, a meeting was convened by the Alderman in the Church to agree upon an assessment for the repair of glass windows and other 'needful things about the church'. Nearly two years later some townsmen had refused or delayed payment of their assessment towards the repairs 'whereby great losses have beene and likelye is to be yf some speedy course be not taken to prevent the same'. Late payers or refusers were to be distrained if they had not paid their share within a month. It was also noted that 'Great abuse & hurte' was done to the leads and other parts of the church upon Shrove Tuesday by people climbing up the church tower which was accordingly forbidden. Despite the threat of distraint, contributions were slow in coming in and alternative ways of effecting the repairs were resorted to. In December 1648, a joiner, Richard Davie, desired to be made free which was granted on condition that 'he should keep and maintain all the wainscoat belonging to pews and seats in the church for 7 years'. The church chancel was reported in September 1647 as 'much decayed & in danger of falling yf not timely prevented' and it was agreed that it should be viewed to estimate the cost of repairs and to send to the prebends for the speedy repair of it.[50]

A more serious problem faced the Corporation in July 1652 when a breach was made in the steeple by thunder and lightning such that the upper part of the steeple 'must be taken downe' and an assessment of £30 was agreed (Figure 9).[51]

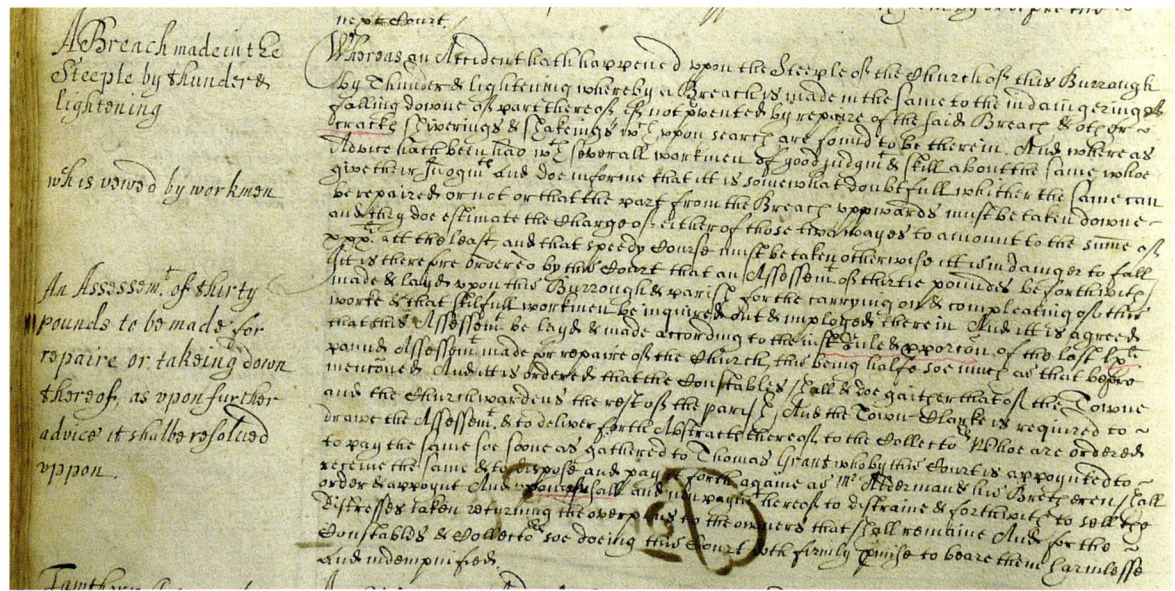

Fig.9 Agreement for repairs to the steeple 16 July 1652 - Folio 252v

Whereas an Accident hath happened upon the Steeple of the Church of this Burrough by Thunder & lightening whereby a Breach is made in the same to the indaingering falling downe of part thereof if not prevented by repaire of the said Breach & other crackes shiverings & shakeings which upon search are found to be therein. And where as Advice hath been had with severall workmen of good judgment & skill about the same whoe give their Judgments and doe informe that itt is somewhat doubtfull whither the same can be repaired or not or that the part from the Breach uppwards must be taken downe and they doe estimate the Charge of either of those two wayes to amount to the summe of xxx li att the least, and that speedy Course must be taken otherwise itt is in dainger to fall Itt is therefore ordered by this Court that an Assessement of thirtie poundes be forthwith made & layd upon this Burrough & parish for the carrying out & compleating of this worke & that skilfull workmen be inquired out & imployed therein And itt is agreed that this Assessement be layd & made according to the instant Rule & proporcion of the last lx li pound Assesemt made for repaire of the Church, this being halfe soe much as that before mencioned And itt is ordered that the Constables shall and doe gaither that of the Towne and the Churchwardens the rest of the parish And the Town Clarke is required to drawe the Assessement & to deliver forth Abstractes thereof to the Collectors Whoe are ordered to pay the same soe soone as gathered to Thomas Grant who by this Court is appoynted to receive the same & to dispose and pay it forth againe as Mr Alderman & his Bretheren shall order & appoynt And upon refusall and non payment hereof to distraine & forthwith to sell the Distresses taken returning the overplus to the owners that shall remaine And for the Constables & Collectors soe doeing this Court doth firmly promise to beare them harmlesse and indempnified.

Distraint of goods for any refusers and non-payers was agreed from the outset. The £30 proved insufficient and a further £15 assessment was agreed in September 1652. Constables in every ward were directed at regular intervals to chase up non-payers and were even threatened with being distrained themselves for not having gathered in the monies. The church remained without the top of the steeple for a decade until repairs were completed in 1664 as evidenced by the list of benefactors in the Ringing Chamber.[52] Despite its good intentions, the Corporation appears to have been unable to gather the resources to fully restore the church; this is perhaps not surprising given the assessments raised for other priorities and the general level of indebtedness that the Corporation found itself in during the 1650s.

8. The Grammar School

The origins and early history of the school (Figure 10) have been described by Sam Branson and the Letters Patent that set out its foundation as the King's School are reproduced elsewhere.[53] These granted to the Corporation the lands and tenements of the former chantries of Holy Trinity and of the Blessed Mary together with rents from four further properties formerly used to keep obits or anniversary prayers. The stated aim of this was that the Free Grammar School 'may be better maintained to endure for all times'. The school's estate in 1553 had a stated value of £14 3s 3d and the Corporation had to pay 16s 8d annually to the Crown. The Alderman and Burgesses were also required to find at their own cost 'a suitable, honest, able and literate person,

Fig.10 King Edward VI's Grammar School, Grantham

well instructed and learned in Latin and Greek letters diligently to serve the said Free Grammar School,' who should have out of the said lands a salary of £12 a year. In managing the school and appointing the schoolmaster, the Corporation should take the advice of Sir William Cecil or after his death the bishop of the diocese or, if vacant, the Master of St John's College in Cambridge. Accordingly, a century on from these Letters Patent, the Corporation essentially had two key roles as regards the school – appointing the schoolmaster and managing the lands that formed the endowment. In January 1649, the Corporation appointed John Birkett but there appears to have been some dissatisfaction over his performance within a matter of months as the Corporation wrote in April to a Mr Kempe in Hitchin to see whether he would be willing to become schoolmaster but he was 'not willing to remove'. In June the Corporation enquired of a possible schoolmaster in Essex but the outcome is not recorded in the Hall Book. In July it was agreed that Birkett should continue 'to the breaking upp before Christide'.[54] On 7 December as Christmas rapidly approached, 'upon debate & consultacion of the whole Court, It was concluded upon that he should not be continued Schoole Master of the Free Schoole of Grantham any longer.' At their first meeting after Christmas the Court was informed that Mr Stokes, schoolmaster at Melton, was a very able man 'every way qualified' and that he had been conferred with about coming to Grantham. It was noted that there were many knights and gentlemen of quality near about who would send their children to a free school if it were provided of an able man for teaching. The Court agreed to choose Henry Stokes on an annual salary of £20 with 20 nobles from Corpus Christi College, Oxford, and under the same conditions

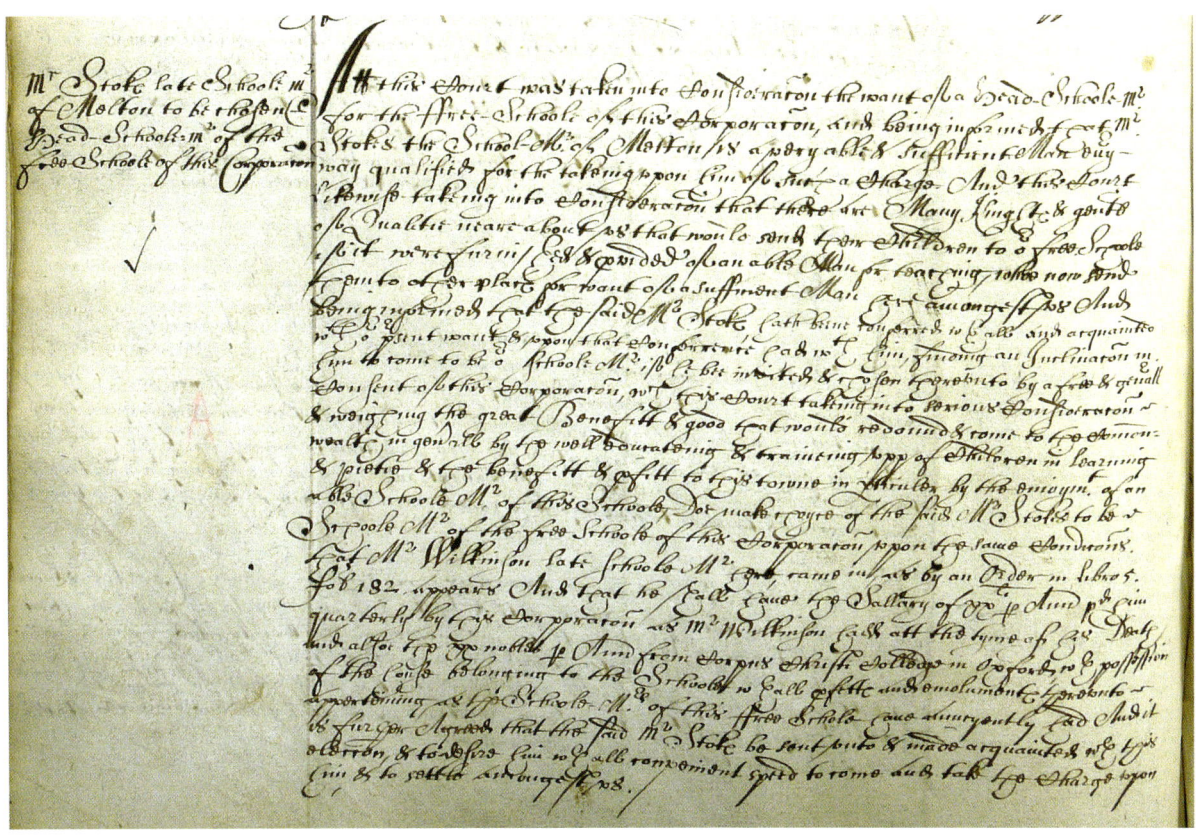

Fig. 11 - Appointment of Henry Stokes, Schoolmaster 11 January 1650 - Folio 208v

as enjoyed by Mr Wilkinson, schoolmaster from 1605 to 1645. Stokes came to the Court on 1 February and formally accepted the offer with all thankfulness and 'promised to bestow his paynes & utmost Endeavours for the Improvement of this Schoole, whereby he might bring glory to God, and benefitt to this Corporacion'. It was made clear that the appointment was to continue at the Corporation's pleasure with his continuance upon Stokes' 'good behaviour, Orderly Method of teaching & sufficiency for learning and knowledge' (Figure 11). Stokes clearly settled in well and made his mark and he remained at the school until 1663 throughout the period that Isaac Newton attended the school.

Contemporary with Stokes, the school's usher or second master was William Clarke's half-brother, Joseph, appointed in June 1649. He continued as usher until 1662. The largely Puritan Corporation was thus ensuring that both the master and the usher were of a similar persuasion to their own beliefs and values.[55]

The management of the lands and properties with which the school was endowed appears to have largely fallen to the two Collectors of School-house rents who were appointed annually. One was usually a Comburgess and the other a Commoner or member of the Second Twelve. The gathering in of rents at Michaelmas and Lady Day no doubt brought the usual problems - some tenants were in arrears and where they had died there was a need to deal with executors and administrators and some properties had fallen into disrepair and had become difficult to let. Some Collectors seem to have been more effective or fortunate than others as the amounts reported as having been collected varied from £43 18s in 1650-51 to £46 14s 8d in 1660-61. Expenditure on the salaries of the master and usher and other outgoings varied between £40 6s 8d in 1652-53 and £46 7s 3d in 1660-61.[56]

A more systemic problem existed in maintaining a central record or terrier to show what leases, whether part of the school estate or of other property held by the Churchwardens or the Chamberlains, were coming up for renewal and when and what opportunities might exist to review rents and increase them in line with inflation. Some Aldermen appear to have been more proactive in managing the Corporation's properties. During William Clarke's second term as Alderman on 3 July 1657, 'Mr Cony brought in a catalogue or list of all the town's land both in and out of lease' amounting to £1,264 16s 8d for entry fines alone. At the same Court it was agreed that for the time to come no lease should be let for above 21 years and that no lease be let until within five years of the expiry of the old lease.[57] Although the Collectors were responsible for the collection of rents, it was the full Corporation that agreed the granting and renewal of leases. For example, in September 1653, it was agreed that Robert Lewin should have a lease of the 'house where he lives in Vine Street for one & twenty yeares from Lady day last (if he and Bridgett his wife soe long live) under the Rent of xv s per Annum and a Couple of Hens yearly att Christide'. He was to pay an entry fine of £6 13s 4d in two instalments. The house stood on the corner of Vine Street and Elmer Street where 10 Vine Street now stands. Lewin was a baker and died in 1670. The young Isaac Newton would have walked past this bakery on his way to school (Figure12).[58]

The terms of the Corporation's leases included a range of covenants including for non-payment (which could lead to ejection and repossession), for repair (usually the tenant's responsibility although sometimes including provision for the tenant to repair or partially rebuild in consideration for a reduced rent) and also for tenants to grind their grist at the town's mills.

By the 1660s, Corporation properties were generally being re-let for the term of 21 years to existing tenants at the expiring rents and for the same or indeed lower entry fines. John Coates was granted a lease of his house in Castlegate for 21 years with a £4 fine and covenanted to rebuild it with stone walls by Michaelmas next. Perpetual renewal of properties at the outgoing rents and with the same fines was to lead to problems in the late eighteenth century when the Corporation's income from the estate was insufficient for the school's expenditure and salaries. This ultimately led to a prolonged case in Chancery and a private Act of Parliament in 1816 for the sale of the school estate.[59]

9. Other corporate responsibilities

The Alderman's Court and the Corporation members and officials took responsibility and regulated many aspects of life in Newton's Grantham. It is worth remembering that, whereas we now live in a society with several layers of local government at county, district and parish levels, supplemented by a range of other agencies such as health and environmental authorities the

Fig.13 The Conduit, Market Place, Grantham

burgesses of Grantham looked to the Corporation to provide all essential services and what would now be termed the town's infrastructure. Adequate supplies of drinking water were obtained from the Conduit situated in the Market Place (Figure 13) that had supplied the town with water from Barrowby since the early fourteenth century. The water came through lead pipes and this was kept in repair through a contract with a plumber, William Palmer, who had served his apprenticeship in the town and was made free in November 1649. This contract, which was to run for seven years, provided that Palmer should maintain (at his own charge) and keep in good tune and repair the Conduit for so much as concerned 'plumber work' and he was to be paid 30s a year. The arrangement appeared to have worked as it was 'againe agreed with Wm. Palmer for 7 yeares more' upon the same terms and conditions in May 1658 (Figure14).[60]

Supplementing the Conduit in the Market Place were public wells in High Street, Market Place, Swinegate and Westgate wards which were maintained and repaired though specific assessments in the relevant wards and collected by the Constables. Westgate inhabitants had to find 30s for repairs to their well in October 1650 and a month later the Swinegate well needed 20s for repairs. The former constables for that ward were being chased for these assessments in November 1651. Within two years the same well needed 30s for repairs which was to be raised from Swinegate and Walkergate. From time to time, the Hall Book records that overseers were appointed for wells; for example, William Baly and Steven Simpson were given charge of Westgate well in October 1652.[61]

The upkeep of pavements and the town's roads was an ongoing topic in the Alderman's courts. Householders were expected to clean the streets in front of their houses and pave up to four yards in front of their doors. The Constables of each ward were charged with reporting those who had not complied. Removal of refuse and keeping the streets clean particularly around the times of fairs was seen as a priority.[62] The Great North Road from London to York by way of High Street and Walkergate had the heaviest wear. In October 1650, the Court agreed repairs with stone being sought from the villages in the soke of Grantham which were also asked for assistance in transporting the stone back to the town (Figure15).[63]

In terms of content within the Hall Book, matters relating to the town's mills appear to have occupied more time at the Alderman's Court than the roads and water supply combined. The Slate (or North) mill at the northern extremity of the town lay close to the Mowbeck's confluence with the River Witham and the Well Lane (or Wellam) Mill, also known as Queen's Mill or South Mill, lay at the end of the road which is now known as

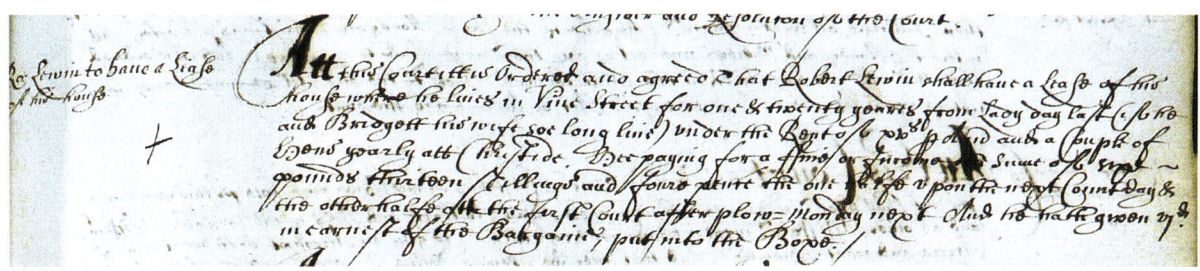

Fig.12 Agreement for lease of Robert Lewin's house in Vine Street 2 September 1653 – Folio 264r

31

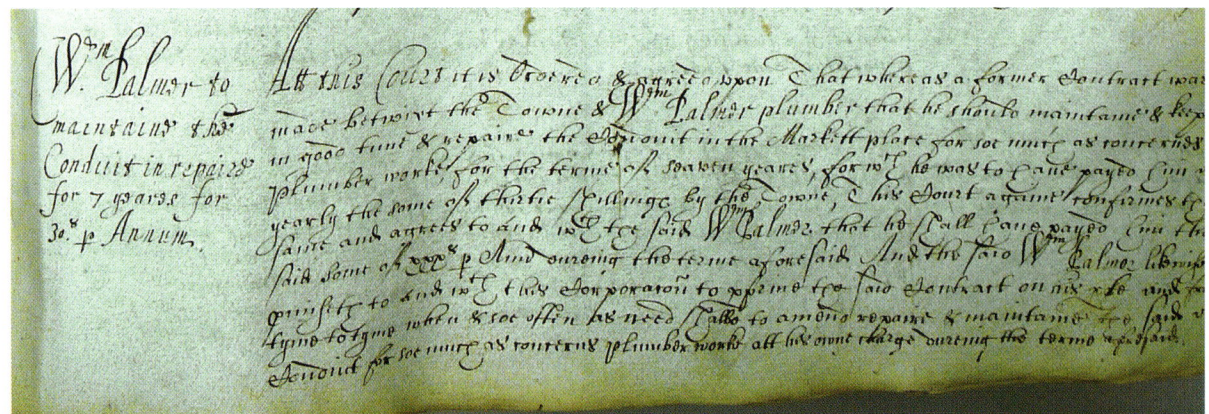

Fig.14 Agreement for maintenance of Conduit by William Palmer 1 February 1650 - Folio 209r

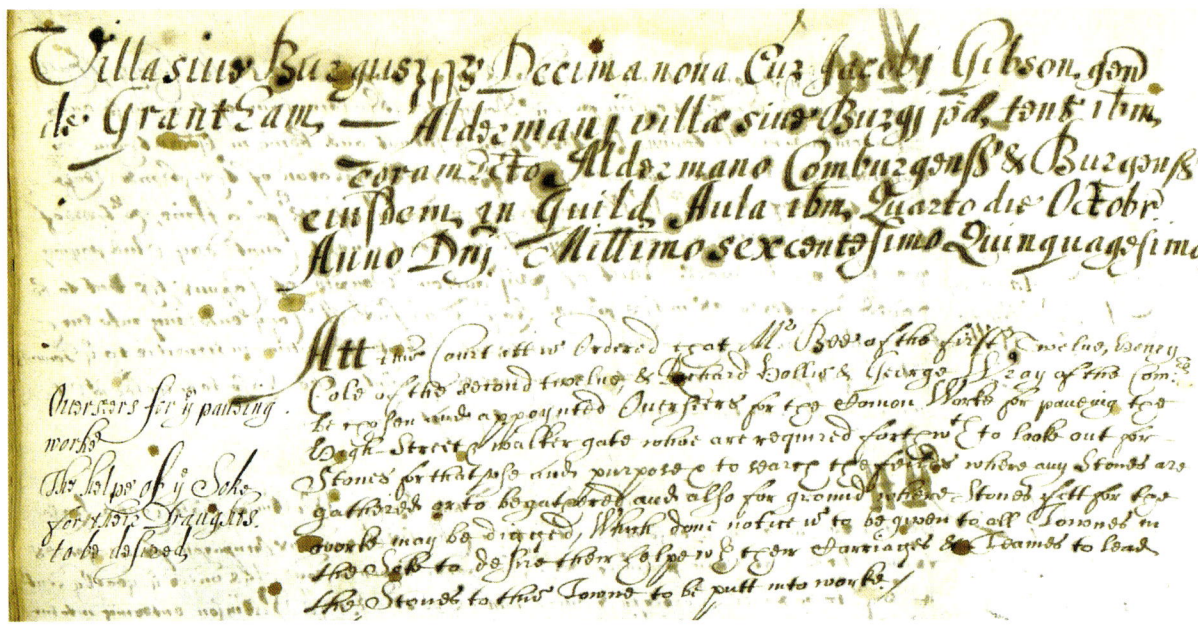

Fig.15 Agreement for repairs of streets 4 October 1650 - Folio 217v

East Street. Each mill had two pairs of mill-stones probably powered by separate mill-wheels fed by the mill-streams drawn from the Witham. The freehold of the mills formed part of the manor which since the later medieval period had been in the hands of the crown where it usually formed the jointure or dowry of the Queen, hence the Queen's Mill. The crown generally leased out the mills which were then sub-let to millers. In 1590, Elizabeth I, on the advice of Lord Burghley, leased the 'two water-mills called Wellam Mills' and a small close containing one and a half acres to the Alderman and Burgesses of Grantham at an annual rent of £6 13s 4d.[64]

In 1610, the crown disposed of both mills to two London merchants who conveyed them in trust to a group of five Comburgesses and two burgesses 'to the proper use and behoof of the Alderman and Burgesses of Grantham'. Accordingly, the Corporation, during the time that Newton went to school in Grantham, was the owner and operator of the mills that had a monopoly on the grinding of grain within the town. The requirement of tenants to use the mills was, as we have seen, enforced through covenants in town leases. Constables and the loadsmen who worked at the mills reported on those who ground at other mills and delinquents were distrained accordingly (Figure 16). Given that bread was an essential and staple part of the diet of the town's residents, the effective management of the mills for the common good to ensure adequate supplies of flour was a key objective of the Corporation.[65]

The mills thus provided the borough with much needed revenue. The management of the Mills was down to the Mill-Masters and the Hall Book gives some detailed accounts showing that the mills could achieve a small profit.[66] When the town agreed to borrow £2000 from Mr Welby, Mr Clarke, Mr Trevillian and Mr Hurst, it was the income from the Mills that was used to pay the interest on the loan. Nevertheless, receipts varied owing to weather conditions and the drought in 1653-54 affected the income and the price of

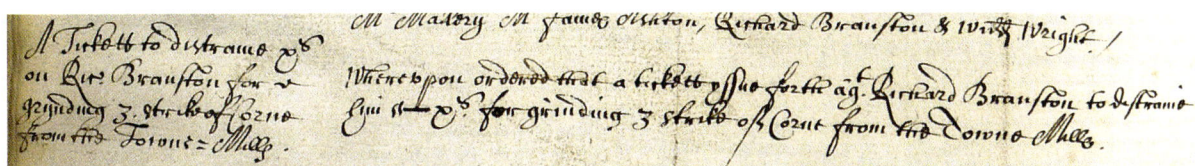

Fig.16 Order to distrain Richard Branston 8 January 1658 – Folio 312v
A Tickett to distraine x s on Ric. Branston for grinding 3. Strike of Corn from the Towne-Mills. Whereupon ordered that a ticket yssue forth against Richard Branston to distraine him x s. for grinding 3 strike of Corne from the Towne Mills.

grain varied as noted in the Hall Book:

"The reason of these 3 Quarters arrers is because of the two last yeares want of Water & also in regard of the great fall of the prises of all sorts of Corne, for when the Agreement was made to pay 200 li per Annum out of the Mills water was plentifull, Mault att 48 s per Quarter and now but at xvi s per Quarter, wheat att 8 s per strike, and now but ii s, Rye at iii s viii d per strike & now but xvi d".[67]

Mills however needed to be maintained with work done to the banks of the Mill streams and river Witham for which a Common day was declared, with every householder charged with finding a day's labour with each ward contributing on a set day.[68] Mill-stones needed to be renewed and the wooden axles, trees and posts required periodic replacement.

A modest annual fee farm rent was however still payable to the Crown even after the Corporation had acquired the mills. In 1650, Parliament needed to raise cash to meet arrears of army pay and Crown lands and the fee farm income from rents and other manorial income was put up for sale. Clarke, then Alderman, responded quickly and persuaded the Corporation to purchase the farm of the mills together with the farm of the Market tolls. It is believed that Grantham was one of only three Corporations that purchased former Crown estates. Richard Cony arranged to purchase the freehold of a house in the Market Place occupied by his daughter but part of the manorial estate and shared the legal costs with the Corporation. It may be argued that the purchase of the market tolls and the fee-farm of the mills would have been to the longer-term benefit of the town had it not been for the restoration of the monarchy in 1660. Clarke also purchased for himself the reversion of the George Inn and adjacent property at a cost of over £1000.[69]

Besides its watermills, the town had a Horse Mill where power was generated by a horse walking in a circle. In 1653, it was agreed to purchase a wind-mill. Although its exact location has not been determined, it may have been on the road towards Gonerby as mentioned in the Memoires of Isaac Newton noted in Turnor's Collections. By May 1657, it was ordered that the wind-mill should be sold.[70]

The Corporation, through its royal charters, had acquired the rights to hold weekly markets and fairs. The Hall Book reveals that in Newton's Grantham the Corporation used a bellman to announce the opening of the market each morning to ensure that no pre-emption or trading prior to the official start took place. Whilst freemen had the right to have a stall, out-of-town stallholders were expected to pay for the privilege; for example, Henry Lambe of Braceby, ironmonger, agreed to pay 6s 8d yearly for his stall in 1654.[71] The markets and fairs were also controlled or supervised by the Alderman and Comburgesses who walked the fair wearing their cloaks. The Escheator ensured that weights and measures were accurate and the Pricers (or Prizers) of corn attempted to ensure that prices of grain were subject to control.

Relief of poverty for the deserving poor was a parish responsibility under the 1601 Poor Law. Parishes elected Overseers of the Poor who collected a poor rate and could distribute relief accordingly. The Corporation assisted individuals by sanctioning collections on their behalf and by remitting assessments in return for taking on poor apprentices. A key objective for the Puritan Corporation was to reduce idleness and set the poor to work. In 1650 the Corporation began attempts to find a wool man or jersey man who would establish a Manufactory in Grantham. Several men were approached and it was agreed to engage William Heacock who was to set up at Dimsdale House, believed to have stood on the site of the present Vicarage. The venture proved abortive; it was noted in September 1653 that Heacock 'had not set the poor on work for above a year now past' and, in July 1654, he was ejected from Dimsdale House. Subsequent efforts from 1656 under Thomas Robinson to set up a Walk Mill appear to have been more successful at first.

By November 1661, the Corporation was trying to relocate Robinson from Dimsdale House but in the Alderman's Court on 31 January 1662 he refused. When Comburgess Thomas Mills asked Robinson what service he ever did for the town. Robinson 'replyed with divers uncivill speeches to Mr Milles....that he had done better service for the Towne then the said Comburgess". The Court then sought security for Robinson's better behaviour and, for want of this, Robinson was committed to the gaol. By September Robinson and family had left the town on entering into an agreement promising not to bring any action against the town.[72]

10. Conclusion

The Hall Book for the period 1649 to 1662 demonstrates the attempts of the Corporation of Grantham to establish and manage a community where certain Puritan values were paramount. The composition of the Corporation had radically changed in 1647 with new faces including William Clarke, Thomas Doughty and Robert Trevillian. They, together with the more experienced Richard Cony, showed reforming zeal and energy as exemplified in the detail of the Hall Book by the sheer number of items dealt with compared with earlier years (Appendix 1).

The objectives of providing Godly ministers and lecturers for the town's spiritual needs and of appointing a suitable schoolmaster were achieved. Significant efforts were made to clean and repair the streets and to maintain the Conduit and these initiatives would have been visible and of benefit to the whole community. The borough's debts may not have been reduced but there had been successful attempts to manage them diligently and to secure a longer-term benefit as exemplified in the purchase of the fee-farm of the mills and tolls. In terms of setting the poor to work and reducing idleness, the measures taken appear to have had limited success. In regard to the reduction of the number of inmates, there is perhaps insufficient evidence to form a judgment.

Whilst it is almost impossible to say with any degree of certainty what Grantham's impact was on Isaac Newton whilst he was attending the Free Grammar School, we may reasonably infer that, as a lodger in the house of such an influential Comburgess and Alderman, living as he did a few doors away from the Guildhall and exposed to Godly teaching at school and in church, the likelihood is that his experiences were formative. It may also be speculated that the schoolboy's experience of the shortage of small change in Grantham and the recognition of the need to issue trade tokens was carried forward into his management of the Royal Mint in later life. In any event, Newton's adult life shows many of the characteristics that were apparent in William Clarke and those who governed Grantham in the 1650s – diligence, attention to detail, energy, zeal and Godliness.

References

1. Lincolnshire Archives (hereafter LA): Grantham Borough 5/1 (hereafter cited as Hall Book)
2. Hall Book fo 208v (11 January 1650) refers to the appointment of Mr Wilkinson as Headmaster of the Grammar School in Book 5. This appointment was made in 1605
3. Turnor, Edmund, 1806, *Collections for the History of the Town and Soke of Grantham*, London
4. Martin, G H (ed.), 1963, *The Royal Charters of Grantham 1463-1688* Leicester 32-33; Hall Book fo 276v (13 October 1654)
5. Pointer, Michael, 1978, *The Glory of Grantham*, Grantham 28-29
6. Manterfield, John B, 1981, *The Topographical Development of the Pre-Industrial Town of Grantham, Lincolnshire, c1535-c1835*, unpublished PhD thesis, Exeter, 141-2; Foster, C W, 1926 *The State of the Church* Lincoln Record Society 23, Lincoln 337-353; Langley, Arthur S, 1920. A Religious Census of 1676 A.D. *Lincolnshire Notes and Queries* 16.2, 33-51
7. LA: BNLW 1/1/35/398 lease of Pest House; Hall Book, for example, fo 206v (16 November 1649) and 207r (7 December 1649)
8. *Privy Council Registers in Facsimile I-1637*, 1967, 97-98
9. Martin, 1963, 14-25; Manterfield, John, Grantham in the later Medieval period, in Start, D and Stocker, D (eds) 2011, The *Making of Grantham – the medieval town*, Heckington, 39-50
10. Martin, 1963, 71-83 and 97-107
11. Martin, 1963, 109-119; Hall Book fo 237r (17 October 1650)
12. Martin, 1963, 120-155
13. Welby, A C E, 1906, *Records of the Parish and Prebendal Church, the Guilds and Chantries of Grantham*, Grantham, 17-18
14. Hall Book fos 206v (16 November 1649); 323r (17 December 1658) and 332r (11 May 1660)
15. Hall Book fo 226r (3 January 1651)
16. Hall Book fos 231v (6 June 1651) and 273r (21 April 1654)
17. Martin, 1963, 136-9
18. Rutland, Emma, Duchess of, 2009, *Belvoir Castle*, London, 30-31
19. Couth, Bill, 1995, *Grantham during the Interregnum - The Hall Book of Grantham 1641-1649*, Lincoln Record Society 83 (hereafter (LRS)), 96-97; http://www.historyofparliamentonline.org/volume/1660-1690/member/ellys-%28ellis%29-william-1607-80 Ellis William 1607-80; Hall Book fo 360v (30 January 1662)
20. Couth, Bill, 1995, *"Crocadiles ffrench flies and other Animalls" Grantham at peace and war 1633-1649* Nottingham; Couth (LRS) 1995
21. Couth (LRS) 1995, 62-63 & 91-97; Hall Book fos 223r (1 November 1650), 241r (31 October 1651) and 258r (30 October 1652) Doughty had serverd Richard Cony as an apprentice.
22. Hall Book fos 300r (31 October 1656); 310r (30 October 1657) and 321r (29 October 1658)
23. Hall Book fos 345r & v (22 March 1661); 348v (14 June 1661); 353r (3 October 1661); 354v (24 October 1661) and 365v and 366r (27 August 1662)
24. Halliday, Paul, 1998, *Dismembering the Body Politic - Partisan Politics in England's Towns 1650-1730* Cambridge; Underdown, David, 1992, *Fire from Heaven - Life in an English Town in the Seventeenth Century*, New Haven and London, provides a case study of Dorchester
25. Foster, C W (ed.), 1916, *The Parish Registers of Grantham in the County of Lincoln 1562-1632* Lincoln Record Society – Parish Register Section IV, Horncastle
26. Couth, 1995 (LRS), 100, (8 October 1647) – it was agreed the First Twelve should not walk abroad in the town without their cloaks on pain of 12d and that the Alderman should wear his gown; Hall Book fo 301v (23 January 1657) – William Clarke was Alderman when the Order of 1647 was repeated; fo 237r (17 October 1651) – again Clarke was serving his first term as Alderman when the order was agreed that the Bell Man should give notice regarding the selling of distresses.
27. For a general discussion of the role of corporate towns and relationships with central government, see Patterson, Catherine F, 1999, *Urban Patronage in Early Modern England – Corporate Boroughs, the Landed Elite and the Crown 1589-1640*, Stanford, California, and Clark, Peter and Slack, Paul, (eds.), 1970, *Crisis and Order in English Towns 1500-1700* London; The Stamford Freeman's oath is printed in Tebbutt, Laurence, 1975, *Stamford Clocks and Watches* 43; Examples of this wording for the election of Alderman are fo 320r (22 October 1658) and for admissions of

freemen fo 313v (19 February 1658)
28. Hall Book fo 213r
29. Hall Book fo 287r
30. Hall Book fos 207v (24 December 1649) and 304r (undated – May 1657)
31. Couth, 1995 (LRS), 136-8
32. Hall Book (passim) fos 258r-288v
33. Townsend, T W, 1983, *Seventeenth Century Tradesmen's Tokens of Lincolnshire The Issuers*, Lincoln
34. Hall Book fos 287r (21 September 1655) and 287v (5 October 1655)
35. Hall Book fos 211v (5 April 1650); 236r (26 September 1651) and 301v (23 January 1657)
36. Hall Book fo 281r (10 November 1654); University of Nottingham MSS, Pl E9/1/36 (the Company of Shoemakers paid 10s yearly to the Manor of Grantham for their privileges); National Archives: E317/Parliamentary Surveys Lincolnshire/19
37. Manterfield, 1981, 258-9
38. Hall Book fos 331v (11 April 1660); 342r (11 January 1661) and 344v (6 March 1661)
39. Hall Book fo 19v (18 July 1635); Manterfield 1981 144-146
40. Couth 1995 (LRS), 129 (20 April 1649)
41. Hall Book fos 284r (2 March 1655) and 302r (13 February 1657)
42. Street, Benjamin 1857, *Historical Notes on Grantham and Grantham Church*, Grantham 84-90; Couth, 1995, (Crocadiles, ffrench flies and other animals) 26-30: For the Grantham Altar controversy in its wider context, see Fincham, Kenneth and Tyacke, Nicholas, 2008, *Altars Restored: The Changing Face of English Religious Worship 1547 - 1700* Oxford.
43. Couth; 1995,(Crocadiles, ffrench flies and other animals) 101-106
44. Manterfield, 1981, 95-102 and 182-185; Couth, 1995, (Crocadiles, ffrench flies and other animalls) 79, 93, 103-104
45. Couth, 1995 (LRS), 70
46. Street, 1857, 1995 (LRS) 136
47. Couth, 1995, (Crocadiles, ffrench flies and other animalls), 191; Couth 1995 (LRS), 74 and 128; Hall Book fo 218v (12 July 1650)
48. Hall Book fos 209v (7 January 1650); 210r (1 March 1650); 214v (12 July 1650); 227r (6 February 1651) and 228v (7 March 1651)
49. Street, 1857, 82-83; Hall Book fos 269v (18 November 1653) and 367av (19 September 1662)
50. Couth, 1995 (LRS), 46, 77, 95 and 125
51. Hall Book fo 252v (16 July 1652)
52. Hall Book fo 254r (17 September 1652); Street 1857, 79-80
53. Branson, S J, 1988 *A History of the King's School, Grantham ... 660 years of a Grammar School* Gloucester; Martin, 1963, 71-83
54. Couth, 1995 (LRS), 127-132
55. Hall Book fos 207r (7 December 1649); 208v (11 January 1650) and 209r (1 February 1650); Branson, 1988, 27-18, 27-28
56. Hall Book fos 238v (23 October 1651); 266r (20 October 1653) and 357v (1 November 1661)
57. Hall Book fo 304v (3 July 1657)
58. Hall Book fo 264r (2 September 1653)
59. Hall Book fo 344r (1 March 1661); 1981, Manterfield, 1981; 85-95 and 173-181.
60. Hall Book fos 206v (16 November 1649); 209r (1 February 1650) and 315r (7 May 1658)
61. Hall Book fos 225r (8 October 1650); 225v (29 November 1650); 243r (7 November 1651) and 259r (29 October 1652)
62. Hall Book fos 206v (6 November 1649); 207r (7 December 1649) and 210r (1 March1650)
63. Hall Book fo 217v (4 October 1650)
64. Martin, 1963, 241-247; Manterfield, 1981, 74-78
65. Hall Book fo 312v (8 January 1657)
66. Hall Book fo 224v (1 November 1650) and 243v (7 November 1651)
67. Hall Book fo 276r (22 September 1654)
68. Couth, 1995 (LRS), 94 (28 September 1647)
69. Manterfield, 1981 165-170
70. Hall Book fos 270v (9 December 1653); 271r (17 February 1653); 273r (21 April 1654); 275r (18 August 1654); 302v (6 March 1656) and 304r (17 April 1657); Hall Book fos 232v (4 July 1651) and 306r (28 August 1657); Turnor, 1806, 176-177
71. Hall Book fo 276v (13 October 1654)
72. Hall Book fos 212v (7 June 1650); 215r (12 July 1650); 215v (12 August 1650); 262v (10 June 1653); 263v (15 July 1653); 274v (28 July 1654); 307r (13 October 1657); 311v (13 November 1657); 360r - 366v (passim) (1662).

Appendix 1- Courts and Assemblies

Year beginning	Alderman	Pages	Items	Courts	Assemblies
1633	Mills J	20	59	12	3
1634	Andrew	21	50	14	1
1635	Cony	29	101	22	2
1636	Archer	15	52	10	4
1637	Sommersall	21	58	16	0
1638	More	26	90	22	1
1639	Pearson	13	61	16	4
1640	Matkin	20	84	19	1
8	*Total 1633-1640*	165	555	131	16
1641	Lloyd	14	61	18	1
1642	Calcroft	8	36	6	6
1643	Christian	13	56	10	3
1644	Mills T	9	31	10	0
1645	Mills/Hanson	16	54	15	0
1646	Cony	48	277	25	2
1647	Briggs	21	100	18	0
1648	Bee	26	165	19	0
8	*Total 1641-1648*	155	780	121	12
16	*Total 1633-1648*	320	1335	252	28
1649	Gibson	34	171	21	0
1650	Clarke	34	160	19	1
1651	Doughty	32	159	20	1
1652	Trevillian	19	117	14	0
1653	Mills T	22	93	15	0
1654	Towne	19	101	15	0
1655	Baily	16	83	11	0
1656	Clarke	20	109	16	0
1657	Doughty	21	93	16	0
1658	Trevillian	13	54	9	0
1659	Simpson	19	74	14	0
11	*Total 1649-1659*	249	1214	170	2
1660	Grant	36	194	22	2
1661	Chantler	25	110	23	1
2	*Total 1660-1661*	61	304	45	3
13	*Total 1649-1661*	310	1518	215	5
29	*Total 1633-1661*	630	2853	467	33

Notes
1. The data for the period 1633-1648 is reproduced from the late Bill Couth's "Crocadiles ffrench flies and other animalls" (1995) 229.
2. The folios in the Hall Book are numbered but some pages jump and others are given the same number. Some pages are left blank and these have been excluded from the above data.
3. The figures for Assemblies exclude the annual Assembly held in St Wulfram's Church on the Friday following St Luke's Day at which the Alderman for the ensuing year was chosen.

Appendix 2 - List of Aldermen, Comburgesses and Second Twelvemen 1649 - 1662

Family Name	Christian Name	Date first appointed Commoner	Second Twelve	Comburgess	Alderman	Date of Dismissal/Resignation/Death	Approx age in 1650
Baily	Thomas	1644	1647-52	1652-61	1655	Resigned 22 March 1661	c30
Bearne	Thomas	1648	1654-62			Resigned 31 January 1662	c23-25
Beck	Nicholas	1645	1652-57	1657-61		Dismissed 18 April 1662 paying £5 as fine for resigning	37
Bee	John	c1630	1641-47	1647-55	1648	Dismissed 21 September 1655 having lived at Folkingham 4 years	c41-50
Briggs	George	pre-1630	1636	1644-Aug 1662	1647	Dismissed for not signing oaths 1662	c52
Bristowe	Edward	1636	1647-51	1651-55		Died before 30 March 1654	c35-40
Calcroft	Richard	1653	1657-61	1661-84	1669, 1681	Died before 3 December 1684	22
Calcroft	Robert (senior)	pre-1630	pre-1633	1638-47 & 1661	1642	Dismissed as royalist 1647; restored 1661	55
Calcroft	Robert (junior)	1660	-	1662-1691	1668, 1684 (part)	Died 1691	24
Chambers	Miles	1651	1654-55			Died before 6 April 1655	c23
Chantler	Gilbert	pre-1630	1637-45	1646-47 & 1661-66		Dismissed as royalist 1647; restored 1661; dismissed as in gaol for debt	c40-45
Charles	Edward	1647	1655-57			Dismissed at own request 3 April 1657	36
Christian	Edward	pre-1630	pre-1633	1639-47 & 1661	1643	Dismissed as royalist 1647; restored 1661; resigned 1 Aug 1662 (very ancient)	c40-45
Clarke	William	1635	1646-47	1647-61	1650, 1656	Resigned at request of Commissioners 1661; died 1682	41
Coddington	Edward	1653	1656-63			Died before 31 July 1663	c28
Coddington	John	1654	1662-70	1670-97	1674, 1683	Discharged as had left the town 2 January 1698	17
Cole	Henry	-	1647-55	1655-58		Dismissed 21 October 1658	30
Cole	Robert	1660	1663-72	1672-c1704	1675, 1685, 1695	Died in or after 1704	11
Cony	Richard	pre-1620	pre-1627	c1627-59	1635, 1646	Dismissed (moved to Charterhouse, London) 8 July 1659	c55-60
Cox	Zachary	1656	1659-67			Resigned 18 October 1667; died before 26 April 1675	c26

Surname	First name					Notes	Age
Dalton	Mawrice	1649	1650-57	1657-61		Resigned at request of Commissioners 1661.	c24-40
Doughty	Thomas	1637	1646-47	1647-61	1651, 1657	Died before 3 March 1661	c35-40
Elston	Richard	1649	1650-51			Dismissed 17 October 1651 because indicted for fornication	c32-40
Fearin	John	1646	1652-58	1658-61		Resigned 22 March 1661	c25-30
Ferman	Henry	1640	1644-50	1650-56		Resigned before 22 February 1656	36
Fisher	John	1644	1652-57			Died before 13 October 1657	31
Gibson	James	c1630	1646-47	1647-61	1649	Died before 8 October 1652	c38-42
Grant	Thomas	1644	1648-56	1656-75		Died before 16 April 1675	c32
Grococke	William	1641	1650-55			Resigned 6 April 1655 because of weakness	c30
Hanson	Christopher	pre-1630	1634	1640-50 & 1661	May-Oct 1646	Dismissed as royalist 7 June1650; restored 1661; died 1670	c43-50
Hanson	Thomas	1640	-	1662-70	1665	Died before 20 May 1670	34
Holley	Richard	1647	1655-65	1665-84	1670 (part), 1682	Died before 19 December 1684	c28-35
Humes	Henry	1656	1662-67	1667-80	1672	Died before 6 January 1680	c25
Hutchin	Hugh	1653	1657-66	1666-67		Died before 18 October 1667	c29
Isaack	Robert	-	1647-49			Departed the town before 7 June 1652	c25-40
Leeming	Richard	1661	-	1662-69	1666	Died before November 1669	29
Lenton	John	1640	1655-66	1666-79	1671	Died before 19 November 1679	c31-35
Mills	Thomas	pre-1630	1634	1641-64	1644, 1653, 1664	Died in office 1665	c53-56
Oldfield	Thomas	1653	1656-63			Resigned 26 June 1663	c30-35
Oliver	William	1655	1657-62			Resigned 18 April 1662	c30-40
Parker	William	1646	1651-54			Died before 30 March 1654	c25-40
Pearson	Richard	pre-1630	pre-1633	1636-47 & 1661	1639	Dismissed as royalist 1647; restored 1661	c55-60
Phiper	John	c1630	1646-47	1647-50		Dismissed on request living at Lincoln	c40
Poole	Andrew	1661	1662			Refused to take place on Second Twelve October 1663; died June 1677	30
Poole	John	1655	1658-62			(listed 1 November 1661; took oath but refused to subscribe 27 August 1662)	c30-40

Family Name	Christian Name	Date first appointed Commoner	Second Twelve	Comburgess	Alderman	Date of Dismissal/Resignation/Death	Approx age in 1650
Poole	William	-	1647-54	1654-57		Resigned 14 August 1657 (for his own reasons)	c30
Rawlinson	Edward	1658	1662-67	1667-76	1673	Died before 28 February 1676	14
Rawlinson	John	c1630	1641-47	1647-55		Died before 21 September 1655	c40-45
Rhodes	Arthur	pre-1600	pre-1617	c1617-51	1622	Died before 4 April 1651	c80
Shepperdson	Richard	1646	1648-50	1650-51		Died before 4 April 1651	c30
Short	George	1653	1661-67	1667-72		Died before 18 October 1672	22
Short	Thomas	pre-1630	1661	1661-82	1667, 1679 (part)	Dismissed as royalist 1647; restored 1661	c40-45
Simpson	John	-	1647-55	1655-62	1659	Dismissed 31 August 1662	c33
Speedy	Henry	1644	1647-55	1655-61		Resigned 22 March 1661	41
Tailer	Michael	1648	1654-59	1659-85	1662, 1677	Died before 15 January 1685	c25
Tomlinson	Joseph	1653	1657-62	1662-71	1670	Died before 14 July 1671	c25
Towne	Edward	pre-1630	1637-44	1650-57	1654	Died before 13 October 1657	c55
Trevillian	Robert	1637	1646-48	1648-61	1652, 1658	Resigned 1661	c40
Walton	Thomas	1652	1656-62			(listed 1 November 1661; took oath but refused to subscribe 27 August 1662)	c30-35
Watson	John	-	-	1662-67		Died before 23 April 1667	c25-40
Wilkinson	Hugh	1648	1650-52			(present at meeting 27 January 1652)	c23-35
Wing	John	1657	1662-70	1670-85	1678	Died before 16 March 1685	16
Wythey	John	1635	1647-50	1650-55		Died before 6 April 1655	c36

WILLIAM CLARKE – THE MAN
Ruth Crook

The Hall Book not only provides us with information about Grantham, but also about individuals living there at the time. William Clarke the apothecary and Isaac Newton's landlord, is one such example. The book provides us with facts about the role Clarke played in the town, which, with additional information from other records, helps to construct a picture of the man and his legacy.

William Clarke was born in Grantham in 1609 and baptised at St Wulfram's church on 23 April.[1] His father Ralph Clarke was an apothecary and served as Alderman twice. Ralph's large family consisted of three sons and seven daughters, several of whom died in either infancy or childhood, leaving William as the oldest surviving son. They lived in the rooms above the apothecary shop, situated on the High Street, immediately to the north of The George Inn, where the Great North Road passed through the town.[2] Shortly after William's eighth birthday, his mother died, leaving many very young children. His father remarried and, with his new wife Cassandra, had four more children, beginning in 1620 with Benjamin, followed by Rachel, Joseph and Deborah.[3] William grew up not only surrounded by brothers and sisters, who may have looked up to him as their big brother, but by many travellers who must have passed by the shop, and he would have become used to meeting many different people. He may have attended Grantham Free Grammar School. If so, he would have learned Latin, Greek, mathematics and religious studies, whilst working with his father, who taught him the apothecary and alchemy profession. Sick or injured people were brought to Clarke's house to be treated, and some of them stayed there.

When he was 21, William's father died, and as the oldest surviving son he inherited his property, including the well-stocked shop. The inventory shows that, as well as equipment, the shop had plentiful stores, including rock alum, green coppers, brimstone, bay oil, white lead, red lead and sugars. There were liquorice, rhubarb, almonds, rice, starch, pepper, prunes, raisins, currants, hops and honey, oils of cinnamon, cloves and nutmeg, as well as flowers of rosemary, rose, celandine, gilly flowers and hyacinth. Leaves and seeds included lemon pips and pine nuts, amongst others. There were also soups of lemon and raspberries, juices of dragon's blood, and body parts of crocodiles, French flies and other animals, and minerals and perfumes. The shop also contained scales, weights, measures, shelves, four mortars and pestles of brass, one stone mortar with a wooden pestle, the shop boards and other implements. The rest of the building above the shop was substantial, and had at least two further floors and a garret. The rooms included a hall, parlour, hall chamber, middle chamber, two chambers over the shop, gallery, retiring chamber, gallery chamber, alcove, kitchen, stable, still room, little still room and other room, brewery, buttery and kitchen. In the yard were two young pigs and a pig sty. The back yard had a cow, a hay store, and a barn containing wood, buckets, and lathes.[4]

On 2 October 1638, William married Katherine Johnson at St Wulfram's church, and on 22 April 1640 their first son William was baptised, later followed by Elizabeth, who was baptised on 13 March 1642, and Judith, baptised on 16 February 1644.[5] His wife Katherine died prior to 1647, when he married for the second time on 18 July that year, at Buckminster in Leicestershire. His new wife, Katherine Storer, was reputed to have been a beautiful woman. She was the widow of Edward Storer, and mother to Edward, Katherine and Arthur and step-mother to Ann.[6] Katherine and William had three further children, Joseph, who was born between 1648 and 1651, Martha baptised on 28 March 1652, and John, baptised on 27 December 1653. William was also the father figure to his young siblings, some of whom were not much older than his own children. They had many visitors to stay in their house, including friends, acquaintances and travellers. The building must have been full of bustle and noise, both inside and out. William Clarke, like his father and grandfather before him, had become a well-respected apothecary. He must have been a caring man too, since he treated many sick and injured people, some in his own house and would have listened to and dispensed medicines to sick people in his apothecary shop. In May 1653 a stranger was found dead at their house.[7]

The children also met a variety of different people, including Henry More, who was an English philosopher of the Cambridge Platonist school. More, who was five years younger than Clarke, stayed at the Clarkes' house during his visit to Grantham.

William Clarke was a multi-faceted character. He was forceful in his opinions, which he tried to impose on others, and argued with neighbours when they did not agree. Some were frightened of him and feared for their lives. In October 1655, Edward Coddington was censured for uncivil speech in the borough court, claiming that he was uncertain whether Clarke meant to kill him or not, and saying that he was afraid of him.[8]

Clarke was a deeply religious man and staunch supporter of Cromwell and the Puritans. He sometimes argued about his beliefs in the street,

Fig. 17 Site of William Clarke's House, High Street, Grantham

once having a heated discussion with one of his neighbours in Grantham, asking him whether he was for King or Parliament. The man said that he was for both King and Parliament, so Clarke pressed him further for an answer and the man said that he would be for the king with all his heart. Clarke was then reported to have said 'Thou hast a rotten, stinking heart within thee, for if thou wilt be for the King, thou must be for the papists'. In June 1642, he wrote a letter to the Lord Lieutenant of Lincolnshire, criticising the king, for which he was arrested. He said 'When the king went to York that if the prince had stayed behind him, he should have been crowned king, and now that the prince was gone with the king, the Duke of York should be crowned king'. Clarke was taken to London and his case discussed in Parliament, but was not taken any further because of the outbreak of the Civil War.[9] During the Commonwealth, as Alderman and a Justice of the Peace, he conducted marriages in St Wulfram's church and in churches in the Vale of Belvoir, which enabled him to be in contact with other Puritans in the area. He may even have been part of an intelligence network.[10]

On 24 March 1643 Royalist troops stormed Grantham and took 250 prisoners to Newark. Ninety gentlemen and fifteen townsmen, including William Clarke, were charged with high treason and were due to be tried on 11 April. Grantham was taken for Parliament by Oliver Cromwell in May and 45 royalists were captured. These were exchanged for the prisoners at Newark, who were freed on 22 May.[11]

In the Grantham Corporation minutes of 1645, William is listed as a Commoner and by the end of the first Civil War in 1646 had been elected to the second twelve of the council. In the following year he was elected to the first twelve, a process which had taken him two years, but would normally have taken ten. It was an important step, and a necessary pre-condition for the important role he took in the life of the town and its district during the Commonwealth and the Cromwellian ascendancy of the following decades. As a perfectionist, during his two stints as Alderman in 1651 and 1657, he insisted that things were done properly. He insisted that the Comburgesses wore their cloaks in the town, the town Constables carried their staffs, and that dogs were kept on leads. Scarlet cloaks were also made for the town's musicians. He was also sometimes slow to re-pay his debts and he amassed a large amount of property. In 1658, he was still in arrears with rent on the mill pingle, so it was agreed that he would give the Rev Humphrey Babington the £3 still owed to him by the court and that the remainder of Clarke's debts should be given to the chamberlain.[12] He was clearly very careful with his money, claiming extra expenses from the court as well as being tardy in paying his debts. Yet, he was also a generous man, lending money to the town when they were in need in 1649, at a low rate of return, plus the profits of the town mills. He also lent the town money to pay the vicar Thomas Dilworth, in lieu of tithes.[13]

Clarke was a family man who supported his relations, even if their religious beliefs differed from his. During his second period as Alderman, he managed to persuade the members of the Puritan borough court to employ his brother-in-law, Rev Humphrey Babington, a royalist, as minister of Grantham for six months. He also managed, in 1657, to secure for him the tithes owed and six months' pay. Clarke claimed £3 from the court towards his expenses for going to London 'about Mr Babington's business'.[14] Six years earlier in 1651, Clarke, along with William Bury, a solicitor, had managed to persuade the London Mercers' Company to donate a share from a bequest of a will to provide Grantham with a Godly minister.[15]

In 1655, the 12 year old Isaac Newton came to live in the Clarke household. He boarded in the garret of the house, where Clarke's large library was kept. Newton had been sent to the Grammar School in Grantham from his home in Woolsthorpe, eight miles away. As Newton's landlord, he seems to have been very tolerant, allowing him to draw on the walls, ride around the corridors on his cart and fly kites from his roof-top. It is unclear whether he reprimanded him for being peevish with his step-children over food and fighting after school, since he seemed to insist on good manners.[16] Clarke was a scholar and collected a large library, which he allowed Newton and the children to use. He was certainly a role model for Newton, being the first father-figure that he had known. The children who lived with William Clarke learned from him. He taught them about alchemy and the apothecary trade. They watched him make pills and potions, and learned what herbs and tinctures were used for various illnesses. Newton made extensive entries in his notebook on how to make pills and potions and how to treat sick people.[17] Although only boys were usually given an education during this period, Clarke was enlightened; his daughters could also read and write and he may also have taught them alchemy and apothecary skills.[18]

Clarke was forward thinking too, and was party to the decision to build a windmill on Gonerby Hill, which, it is said, he observed being built with the young Newton.[19] He came back to Clarke's house and made drawings of its construction, mostly on the walls of his room. He built a model windmill, which he placed on the roof of the house to enable it to catch the wind. According to Stukeley, the drawings were lost when the house was rebuilt in 1711, and the windmill had been demolished by 1727.

It is also known that Clarke travelled to Cambridge, Lincoln and London, sometimes on official business and sometimes visiting family and friends. He provided trade tokens for use as small change, and possibly as a means of an early insurance policy, so that people could utilise his services as apothecary. The tokens had the initials W and K Clarke, William and Katherine, referring to his second wife.[20]

After the Restoration of the Monarchy in 1660, the Puritan members of the Corporation were gradually removed from office and William Clarke and Maurice Dalton were asked to leave and resigned in October 1661.[21] William and Katherine and the younger members of their family left Grantham in the 1660s and went to live in Loughborough in Leicestershire, where William died in 1682.[22]

William Clarke can be remembered as a man who worked hard for his town. He tried to introduce new ideas, whilst following his religious ideology. He was forceful in his beliefs and vocally very persuasive in an attempt to impose them on others. He was scholarly and hugely influential on his children and step-children, many of whom followed in his professional footsteps. He was also very generous, lending money to the town, but could be slow in paying his debts. He was a man of contradictory attitudes and behaviour. He is likely to have been hugely influential on the young Isaac Newton, and may have been instrumental in stimulating his interests.

References

1 St Wulfram's church records
2 Royal Society Library, London, MS/142, available at www.newtonproject.sussex.ac.uk
3 St Wulfram's church records
4 Lincolnshire Archives, INV/136/503
5 St Wulfram's church records
6 Bunny and Buckminster church records
7 St Wulfram's church records
8 Hall Book, fo 288
9 *House of Commons Journal*, vol. 2 (1640-43), 27 June 1642, 640-43; *HMC Portland Papers* MSS, I, 40; *The Private Journals of the Long Parliament 2 June to 17 September 1642*, edited by Vernon F Snow and Anne Steele Young, 136-7, 142
10 Bodleian Library, Rawlinson MS 25, fo 33, printed in White, R, 1904, Dukery Records, Worksop, 227
11 Manterfield,1981
12 Hall Book, fo 315
13 Couth 1995 (LRS) 74, 128; Hall Book fo 218v (12 July 1650)
14 Hall Book, fo 302.
15 Hall Book fos 209v (7 January 1650); 210r (1 March 1650); 214v (12 July 1650); 227r (6 February 1651) and 228v (7 March 1651).
16 Royal Society Library, London, MS/142, available at www.newtonproject.sussex.ac.uk
17 Royal Society Library, London, MS/142, available at www.newtonproject.sussex.ac.uk
18 Dr Williams's Library, London, Baxter Correspondence Volume IV, fos. 4-25, Ann and James Truman's letter to Sylvester
19 Hall Book, fos 273r and v (21 April and 16 June 1654)
20 William and Katherine Clarke's Trade Token, J G L Burnby and T D Whittet, 'Local Studies of the English Apothecary, Part 2', *Lincolnshire History and Archaeology* 24 (1989), 20-27
21 *Calendar of State Papers Domestic*: Charles II 1660-1,146; Hall Book fo 353r (3 October 1661)
22 Lincolnshire Archives, Wills 1682/ii/465

Aims:

- Ensure that the town's remaining fine or historically interesting buildings are preserved for future generations
- Monitor the upkeep of green spaces and make our own contribution, where appropriate, to their provision
- Keep a watching brief on new developments and make constructive comments on their likely impact on the town's environment
- Encourage sustainable development and refurbishment
- Encourage a vibrant, attractive, economically viable environment in which to work, live and for leisure

Hence our motto: Preserve the good in the old; encourage the good in the new.

Grantham Civic Trust, as it was known then, was formed in the early 1960s by local people who had become greatly concerned about extensive demolition and poorly planned development in the town.

Over the years we have maintained a good relationship with the planning authorities but kept a critical eye on developments. Our Planning Sub-committee reviews significant planning applications which affect historic buildings and other major developments. Our comments are passed to the Planning Department of South Kesteven District Council which makes decisions on proposed developments.

The Society has played a role over the years in achieving listed status for important buildings under threat of demolition. The district council often consults us on major plans and we have attended many meetings, conferences and visits to other towns over the years as part of the planning process.

The Society has been involved in tree planting schemes and has carried out small scale landscaping projects. The Society was instrumental in the formation of the Rivercare group which continues to be successful in maintaining and improving the River Witham and keeping the parkland through which the river flows clear of rubbish.

Grantham Civic Society has established a triennial Townscape Awards scheme to encourage good new building, conservation and landscape improvements. Over the years the Society has had a beneficial and steady influence on the development of the town. However, the ravages of the 60s and later decades are still all too evident and have left us with a town centre below the standard one expects from a community the size of Grantham. The challenges of traffic, pollution, and parking all remain perhaps in ways different from past times. The District Council is more concerned than ever before not to make the mistakes of the past but there will always be a need for an independent point of view. The Society provides this as long as we represent a large body of informed people.

In recent years the Society has started to erect commemorative Blue plaques to celebrate the lives of famous people who have lived in or passed through the town. Information signboards have been commissioned which graphically explain the history of parts of the town. We believe these things inform townspeople and visitors alike and help to create a sense of place which makes people prouder of their town and perhaps more interested in looking after it.

The Society publishes newsletters, holds speaker meetings, social events and organises visits to places of interest. We host other Civic societies and give guided tours of the town. Our visits elsewhere will often be hosted by another Civic society. Nationally, we are part of Civic Voice which is the national charity for the civic movement which plays a vital part in seeking to influence government policy towards good design and responsible development.

Grantham Civic Society is delighted to be involved with this new book, Newton's Grantham, edited by John Manterfield. The Civic Society has also published two books by Ruth Crook: The History of *Vine House and Vine Street, Grantham* (2013) and *Arthur Storer's World* (2014).

www.granthamcivicsociety.co.uk